Moses Koeningsberg

Southern Martyrs

A History of Alabama's White Regiments during the Spanish-American War

Moses Koeningsberg

Southern Martyrs

A History of Alabama's White Regiments during the Spanish-American War

ISBN/EAN: 9783337339432

Printed in Europe, USA, Canada, Australia, Japan

Cover: Foto ©ninafisch / pixelio.de

More available books at **www.hansebooks.com**

SOUTHERN MARTYRS.

A HISTORY

OF

ALABAMA'S WHITE REGIMENTS

DURING THE

SPANISH-AMERICAN WAR,

TOUCHING INCIDENTALLY ON THE EXPERIENCES OF THE ENTIRE FIRST DIVISION OF THE SEVENTH ARMY CORPS.

BY
SERGEANT M. KOENIGSBERG
Co. E, 2nd Regt. Ala. Vol. Infy.

MONTGOMERY, ALA.
BROWN PRINTING CO., PRINTERS AND BINDERS.
1898.

Entered according to Act of Congress, in the year 1898, by
M. KOENIGSBERG,
In the office of the Librarian of Congress at Washington, D. C.

DEDICATORY.

"*Mors, te salutamus!*" should have been inscribed over the doors of the volunteer army recruiting stations. "Death, we salute thee!" would have been a fitting legend to flutter in funereal folds from every rendezvous where brave men were enrolled on the long list of American victims of a systemless system.

Magnolia and fir trees guard the bones of Southerner and Northerner who succumbed alike in wretched struggles with the results of administrative and executive incompetence. In the noisome camps that stretched at intervals from Mobile to Miami were laid bloodless battlefields where American patriotism contested with American error.

To the unfortunate dead of those unhappy contests, this work is feelingly dedicated in the hope that the truths these pages exploit will aid the erection of a memorial monument on which the mourners' contrition will word itself thus:

"THIS PILE IS TO COMMEMORATE THE ETERNAL DIVORCE OF POLITICS FROM THE ARMY."

Oct. 19, 1898.   THE AUTHOR.

PREFACE.

IT was originally intended by the author to print the names of those Alabamians who volunteered for service and were rejected in the physical examinations. The men who were willing to forsake their civilian interests and share the volunteer's lot are deserving of credit; but letters reaching the historian show that a large number of the rejected patriots are reluctant to have the fact of their ineligibility published. Many appear to smart under the examining surgeons' distinctions. In deference to this spirit and because the author's purpose was to honor rather than embarrass the physically ineligible volunteers, none of their names is published. M. K.

Montgomery, Oct. 19, 1898.

ARGUMENT.

IT may have been an accident that the six regiments selected to suffer at Miami came from Southern States. The author is anxious that the title, "Southern Martyrs," be understood as intending geographical designation rather than sectional significance. There were among the two Alabama regiments many noble Northerners whose eagerness to fight for the Stars and Stripes was greater only than their eagerness to go into battle under Southern officers with Southern comrades.

While the historian does not attempt to fix specifically the blame for the tortures and mortality thrust on the volunteer troops by American mismanagement, it might be well to explain what this narrative purposes to prove. The culpable responsibility rests not only on the military unpreparedness in which the national solons permitted the country to remain for years, but weighs with equal burden in North and South, East and West, wherever political influence was exercised to gain the appointment of incompetent officers.

History ranks in the class of compensatory literature because truth is its essence. "Southern Martyrs" is intended as a truthful narrative. Imagery has been abandoned for accuracy. Such truths in these chapters as may pain individually are calculated to benefit generally through the lessons they teach. And, therefore, though the few comparisons employed may be reckoned by some as odious, though the descriptions given and the facts recited may earn the resentment of some and the gratification of others, the author will feel his object attained if the book succeeds in extending the agitation for a military regimen under which American patriots will cease to suffer such martyrdom as Miami.

To the surviving members of the First and Second Alabama, "Southern Martyrs" may prove useful for souvenir and record purposes. Great pain has been taken to chronicle in unbiased verbiage those incidents that really compose regimental history. Necessarily, many episodes of interest are omitted, because to print all would be practically impossible and to select only some would be as unsatisfactory to the majority of the two regiments as it would be embarrassing to the author.

Unfortunately, some of the facts that the author is most eager to exploit can be confirmed only by the testimony of men yet in the service. To jeopardize the commissions of some or to menace others with the embarrassments of courts-martial is not the purpose of the author. Some of the passages, therefore, in "Southern Martyrs," are guardedly written. None of the statements is exaggerated. At times, where important assertions may lack detail, the absent definiteness may be traced to official records which are as yet guarded in the pigeon-holes of interested officers. Some day, untrammeled by the obligations invested in them by their commissions, a number of these officers will elaborate the averments made in "Southern Martyrs."

Already, before his book has reached publication, skeptical persons—men who wallowed in domestic comforts while fellow-citizens were battling for the nation's welfare—have approached the author with such questions: "But what history can the Alabama regiments have? They saw no active service, and surely regiments in the Civil War suffered more?"

It is in the selfish indifference of such supercilious questioners that the abuses and outrages of America's military methods are fostered and nurtured. If these skeptics would devote more time to a quest for information and less industry in the pursuit of personal pleasures, they might be of political assistance in righting the great wrongs that have been and are being done.

To go barefoot, in tatters, hungry and cold, to toil in the burning sun with torn fingers and emaciated forms, to sleep in the open with no counterpane but Heaven's canopy, to suffer and bleed and famish and endure the harrassings and distresses of unpaid, unfed soldiers in a bloody service—all this is terrible. Americans have experienced such sufferings; Heaven forefend that they shall be again called on to do it. But speaking for the men of the First and Second Alabama, writing for himself who was one of them, the author solemnly declares that rather would they have gone through all the worst struggles of Santiago than have endured one month of Miami.

In "the fierce ecstasy that thrills through manhood's heart of oak when trumpets blow for war" is recompense enough to Americans for all the deprivations of an ordinary campaign. Napoleon's grenadiers grumbled at the inactivity and hardships of Italy, but, once under his master leadership, the horrors of the march to Moscow failed to wring from their lips a single complaint. It is one thing to hear the singing of shot and shell, to see the spattering blood, to catch mind-pictures of ghastly, upturned faces, to quiver and shake in the hellish throb of battle. It is one thing, too, to swelter on long, strength-stealing tramps, to bolt uncooked food, to go, perhaps, half-clothed and worse housed. And it is one thing, too, to know you are doing all this for Old Glory, with true comrades beside you, under courageous and capable leaders, for a grateful nation. The chill of the yawning grave, the fearful whisperings of the flying missiles, the stench, the racking scenes, the sheól of it all becomes one grand epoch of glory in which the proddings of peril, the harassing of hunger and the worry of weariness are merged into a tingle of gratifying excitement.

But, oh! what a different thing it is to grovel in misery at Miami—to toil beyond the limits of human endurance because a blind or criminal officer has been led into a trap and a querulous taskmaster forgets that soldiers are men;

to know that doctors are fighting to rescue you from a hell hole of horrors while incompetent officers, superior in authority, deny the presence of danger; to drink disease germs from day to day because those same incompetent officers withhold you from pure water; to stumble about, bare-foot, in rags, because a prosperous people has failed to appoint men who have energy enough to clothe you out of plethoric coffers; to stifle and swelter, thirsty and weak, through unreasonable and unprofitable drills; to spend the nights battling with mosquitoes and the days contending with insidious death agents; to subsist on illy-cooked food that would of itself have already sent less hardy men to their graves; to slave and have added to your slavery the humiliation of knowing that the men who thrust this martyrdom upon you are protected and favored by the nation you volunteered to fight for.

It is one thing to know you are suffering in a good cause; it is another matter to realize that you are being done to death by incompetents placed above you.

There were, and are, in the First and Second Alabama, as well as throughout the volunteer army, a number of efficient and brilliant officers; but, unfortunately, it was not in their hands that the direction of affairs was vested.

Some scoffers make the puerile, nay childish, argument that the volunteers of 1898 should not complain—that they have no ground for grievance in view of the fact that Confederate and Union soldiers suffered more in the '60's than have the men who served against Spain. How short-sighted are these views! The men who bore the privations and hardships of the Civil War accepted them as a matter of course. There was no overflowing commissary from which the Confederate armies could draw; and the tremendous drain on the coffers of the Northern States had taxed every resource of Lincoln's administration. And the troops were performing the most active service, constantly subjected to the exigencies, losses and inconveniences of interminable contact with hostile forces.

On the other hand, the men at Miami were so far removed from the theater of active operations that they were not even furnished with ball cartridges; they were always in close touch with an undisturbed base of supplies; the energies and activities of a War Department, backed by incalculable means, were supposedly at hand to fill all requisitions; no danger from an armed foe threatened the camp or menaced the commissary; a plan of hardening the volunteers was purposed—and yet the First and Second Alabama need not have suffered more had they participated in the most unfortunate of McClelland's campaigns.

It is difficult then to picture what would have been their fate under similar management in the enemy's country, isolated from their supply depots and dependent upon their surroundings for their subsistence. If men should be trained for war as slaves are led to the galleys; if health is enhanced by disease; if strength comes from exhaustion; if thirst and suffocation and sleeplessness lend endurance; if military morale is obtained through disgust, then the author will become his own apologist and confess that this history is futile and nugatory.

But this explanation could not close with justice unless Mr. Flagler and his pretty coast town of Florida were exonerated from the vituperative assaults of superficial observers. Mr. Flagler has done so much for Florida, he has shown so much sympathy with the soldiers' sufferings, he has given with such unstinted generosity to all the Red Cross and auxiliary causes that one can scarcely believe he countenanced Miami's misery. Miami itself holds forth varied and extensive possibilities of pleasure to the tourist. Superb scenery and magnificent situations lend to the attractiveness of the place and it is easy to live with more than ordinary comfort at the big hotel on Biscayne Bay. As to the responsibility for the mistakes of Miami, the author agrees in a measure with the editor of the Augusta (Ga.) *Chronicle*, who wrote in a September issue of his paper:

"In two and a half years before the camp was established at Miami there had been only one case of typhoid fever. When the soldiers came they bathed in the reservoir and dynamited fish, which rotted in the water supply. But what did the authorities in charge of the troops do? Instead of carting away the offal of the camp daily, it was deposited in sinks near the company wells. The troops were allowed to wash themselves, their clothing, and dishes upon the ground at wells from which they drank water. * * * * Had the troops at Miami been commanded by a wise and firm officer, with any ordinary knowledge of sanitation, there would have been no reasonable complaint. But maledictions were poured upon the Secretary of War for establishing the Miami camp."

That the official careers of the responsible officers are fringed with the graves of Miami martyrs is certainly true. But that the responsibility weighs heaviest with the men who forced the selection of Miami as a camp-site in the face of Gen. J. F. Wade's adverse report, is a fact which will be fully recorded, if not in earthly tribunals, then at that bar where plutocrat and patriot, murderer and murdered meet for eternal judgment. That Gen. J. F. Wade reported Miami, after careful inspection, as utterly unfit for camp purposes is in itself a copious commentary on the subsequent sufferings of the First Division of the Seventh Army Corps.

THOSE WHOM DEATH HAS ALREADY TAKEN.

FIRST ALABAMA.

Hugh Collins, sergeant, Company K, killed at Mobile, Ala., May 3.

Robert J. McCullough, private, Company L, died in division hospital, Mobile, May 27; fever.

Olen J. Olsen, private, Company I, died in division hospital at Mobile, June 9; fever.

V. Walter Smith, sergeant, Company A, died in marine hospital, Mobile, July 15; fever.

J. W. Hannah, private, Company C, died at his home in Gadsden, June 23; fever.

Nicholas P. Gaines, private, Company I, died in marine hospital, Mobile, June 27; fever.

Herman Brada, private, Company M, committed suicide, Miami, July 12.

Charles Schitz, private, Company K, died in division hospital, Miami, August 18; fever.

James M. Stewart, private, Company A, died in division hospital, Miami, August 23; fever.

J. F. Horton, private, Company E, died in division hospital, Miami, August 29; fever.

Philip Neeley Finch, sergeant, Company G, died in division hospital, Jacksonville, August 29; fever.

Captain George F. Hart, commanding Company L, died in St. Luke's hospital, Jacksonville, September 9; inflammation of bowels.

William M. Pride, Jr., private, Company B, died in Florence, Ala., September 20.

William Thompson, private, Company I, died at Opelika, Ala., September 21; complication of ailments contracted at Miami.

W. M. Franklin, private, Company M, died at Hillman hospital, Birmingham, Ala., October 1; dysentery.

Fred Sizemore, private, Company K, died at Hillman hospital in Birmingham, October 3; typhoid fever.

Fred Maloney, private, Company A, died at Birmingham, October 6; apoplexy.

SECOND ALABAMA.

Robert N. Alston, private, Company G, died at Miami, July 23; fever.

L. P. Simmons, private, Company A, died at Miami, August 14; dysentery.

Henry B. McCutchen, private, Company I, died at Miami, August 17; typhoid fever.

W. E. Rollins, private, Company G, died at Jacksonville, August 19; typhoid fever.

Solomon W. Gold, private, Company I, died at Larkinsville, Ala., while home on sick leave; fever.

Anthony Sammereier, private, Company B, died at Jacksonville, August 19; typhoid fever.

J. F. Black, private, Company F, died at Jacksonville, August 24; typhoid fever.

E. E. James, private, Company B, died at Jacksonville, August 26; typhoid fever.

Charles A. McHugh, private, Company C, drowned at Jacksonville, September 2.

Columbus M. Herrin, private, Company E, died in division hospital, Jacksonville, from dysentery contracted at Miami, September 7.

Harmon W. Cox, private, Company C, died in division hospital, Jacksonville, September 10; concussion of the brain.

J. M. P. Hicks, private, Company I, died in division hospital, Jacksonville, September 19; typhoid fever.

Wallace Winborne, private, Company M, killed in railway accident at Montgomery, Ala., September 23.

Robert Tipton, private, Company K, killed in railway accident at Montgomery, Ala., September 23.

Alonzo E. Wells, private, Company B, died at City Infirmary in Montgomery, Ala., October 6; typhoid fever.

This death roll becomes more and more significant as it is studied. Eighteen of the deaths are immediately attributable to ailments contracted during the sojourn of less than five weeks at Miami. This means that a continued stay there would have developed a mortality rate of at least nine in each regiment per month or 216 in the two commands in a year. But surgeons declare that when the order finally came directing a removal to Jacksonville, the "present for duty" men were in such a debilitated condition generally that disease would have found in them a wonderfully rich field. The mortality would have increased as the time passed—if the conditions remained the same—the death rate would have become so appalling as to call forth the indignation of the entire country.

The most sinister element of the situation is the fact that the Moloch of Miami has not yet designated all his victims. Surgeons, whose names are withheld because they are still in the army, have assured the writer that months hence the morbific waters drank in Miami will assert themselves in the illness of numbers of men now apparently in good health. Their theory is simple. It is contained in a diagnosis of Capt. George F. Hart's fatal malady. Part of the water at Miami not impregnated with typhoid germs was rendered brackish by silicate substances that the men frequently discussed but continued to swallow. It is theorized that these silicates accumulate in the abdominal canals and produce calculus.

Capt. George F. Hart's death was generally attributed to ulceration of the bowels. "Miami water killed him," said a surgeon at St. Luke's hospital in Jacksonville, Fla. "And Miami water has not yet finished its work in the First Division of the Seventh Army Corps," said another surgeon whose reputation goes beyond three states. "All its death marks have not yet been tallied." And this prophetic utterance was made September 15, 1898.

FIRST REGIMENT ALABAMA VOLUNTEER INFANTRY.

ELIJAH L. HIGDON, Colonel Commanding.
JOHN B. McDONALD, Lieutenant Colonel.

MAJORS:

First Battalion,	TOM O. SMITH.
Second Battalion,	DANIEL D. McLEOD.
Third Battalion,	OSCEOLA KYLE.

SURGEONS:

Major,	WILLIAM J. KERNACHAN.
First Lieutenant,	LEWIS C. MORRIS.
	(Resigned.)
First Lieutenant,	HARDEE JOHNSTON.
	(Resigned.)
First Lieutenant,	R. M. FLETCHER, Jr.

CHAPLAIN:

Captain,	O. P. FITZSIMMONS.

REGIMENTAL ADJUTANT:

First Lieutenant,	LUCIEN C. BROWN.

REGIMENTAL QUARTERMASTER:

First Lieutenant,	R. M. FLETCHER, Jr.
	(Resigned.)
First Lieutenant,	MORGAN FELIX WOOD

BATTALION ADJUTANTS:

(First Lieutenants.)

First Battalion,	LEON SCHWARZ.
Second Battalion,	P. G. SEAMAN.
Third Battalion,	L. E. BROWN.

NON-COMMISSIONED STAFF:

Sergeant Major,	WALTER E. GARDNER.
Quartermaster Sergeant,	LEWIS W. PATTERSON.

Hospital Stewards, DAVID W. GASS, ROBERT E. HOGAN, and PAUL D. VANN.

MAJ. TOM O. SMITH,
COMMDG. FIRST BATTALION, FIRST REGIMENT ALA. VOLS.

MEN OF THE FIRST ALABAMA.

COMPANY K.
Birmingham Rifles.

CHARLES L. LEDBETTER, Captain.
EDWARD D. JOHNSTON, 1st Lieut.   HENRY T. DEAN, 2d Lieut.
Lieutenant LUCIEN C. BROWN. Transferred to Regimental Adjutant.

Sergeants:

Henry M. Dozier, First Sergeant.
R. Emmett Craddock. Transferred to Band Sergeant.
Walter M. Hagood,
William S. Reynolds,

G. Will Nichols, Q'master Sergeant.
Wm. M. Huey,
Chas. G. Gardner,
Frank M. Barnett, Q'master Sergeant. Discharged.

Corporals:

Ben Catchings,
John E. Ellis. Discharged.
Tom Bowron,
D. O. Robinson,

Charles G. Reid,
Reuben T. Johnston. Discharg'd
Frank L. Moses. Discharged.
Herbert E. Reynolds,

Willie C. Ball, Cook.

Charles F. Morgareidge, Musician.   John Rensford, Musician.
Allen G. Brown, Wagoner. Discharged.
Chas. O. Douthit, Wagoner.

Privates:

Baker, Ernest A. Honorably discharged.
Ballard, Clarence,
Barks, Henry L.,
Ball, Willie C.,
Brown, Reuben J.,
Barnes, Walter,
Brock, Ellis R.,
Brooks, Oliver T.,
Burbridge, Samuel H.,
Butcher, Oscar,

Byers, Edgar B.,
Butler, Mike,
Cowan, A. Sid. Discharged.
Campbell, Goodrich,
Crowder, Geo. A.,
Connolly, Chas. E.,
Cushen, John W.,
Clisby, Warner,
Davis, Ed A.,
Davis, William,
Dyer, Charles,

Endsley, Arthur B.,
Faunce, J. N.,
Francis, Sears,
Fields, Wade H.,
Fowler, Harry,
Fowler, Jack,
Fuller, Allen A.,
Germaine, Pete G.,
Hall, James W.,
Hall, John,
Hathaway, H. Bert,
Havis, Glen W.,
Hicks, Will J,
Hyche, William T,
Huddleston, George,
Hutto, Walter B.,
Jones, Tom R.,
Joseph, Leon,
Keheley, Walter D.,
Kelly, Jeff,
Lamb, William B.,
Latham, John D.,
Lawes, Leo V.,
Leonard, Ernest Eugene,
Lester, Robert E.,
Lockhart, David,
Long, James McK.,
Lytle, J. Fred,
McCaa, Waights,
McCaskey, John P.,
McDonald, Ellis P.,
McDonald, James,
McGrady, Walter,
McKendrick, Allen,
McNulty, John. Transferred to band.
Moore, John W.,
Moser, Gotlieb Aug.,
Napier, John F.,
Oglesby, William S.,
Parrish, Thad,
Patterson, W.,
Perkins, John R.,
Price, Cliff S.,
Raisler, Fred W.,
Randolph, Victor M.,
Ransom, Edgar F.,
Redmayne, Marmaduke,
Reid, Charles G. McD.,
Reed, Sam P.,
Ross, Walter M.,
Russell, Robert L.,
Roebuck, Hamilton D.,
Sizemore, Fred. Dead.
Smith, Fred,
Stewart, Malcolm M,
Sparks, Fred Y.,
Sziepok, Joseph S.,
Taylor, George O,
Terry, Percy W.,
Tambling, Frank,
Webb, Alonzo W.,
Whelan, Patrick C.,
Williams, John,
Zeigler, Thomas R.,
Schitz, Charles. Dead.

Few organizations in the country's national guard have seen more service than Company K (Birmingham Rifles). Its war record is part of Alabama's war record; and its militia history is intertwined in the history of Northern Alabama. After the company's reorganization it was of valuable service in quelling a number of public disturbances. Up to and including the Birmingham riot in 1894, the company manifested the most creditable promptness in responding to every call issued to it. Since then it was summoned to Huntsville, in June, 1897, to save three colored prisoners from mob violence. The company has for years been recognized as a crack military organization and, as a part of Colonel Higdon's regiment, anticipated the call for volunteers in the Spanish-American war by assuring Governor Johnston of a readiness to go to the front at any moment. The officers claim that eighty per cent. of the old membership reported for duty in Mobile in May, the company reaching that rendezvous with ninety-seven men.

The Birmingham Rifles were mustered into the volunteer service on May 9, 1898. Afterward, on June 13, First Lieutenant Lucien Brown was transferred to the regimental adjutantship to succeed Lieutenant Johnston in that office, the latter being relieved at his own request. The company's official personnel was then changed in the manner indicated in the accompanying roster.

Company K gained the mournful prominence of having the first funeral in the regiment, Sergeant Hugh Collins being shot and killed by a negro at Camp Clark, May 3, 1898.

COMPANY L.

Huey Guards (East Lake, Alabama).

GEORGE F. HART, Captain, deceased.
NEWMAN D. LACY, Captain.
JOHN S. CARROLL, 1st Lieut.   GEORGE R. BYRUM, 2d Lieut.

Sergeants:

Andrew J. Lacy, Q'master Sergt.,   Elbert M. Gibson,
William W. Nutt,   Curley H. Self.
John S. Hargrove,

Corporals:

Homer R. Brown,   Herman L. Merz,
John H. Cook,   Smith C. Fuller.
Charles C. Hagin,   Rufus W. Jones,
William W. Lampkin,   August Martin,
George Swanton,   Fred M. Warner,
Edmund D. McCrary,   John J. Burnette.

Charles H. McClaflin, Alonzo G. Worrell, Musicians.

Joseph Wolf, company cook; James H. Worrell, artificer; William D. A. Brown, wagoner.

Privates:

Adams, Joseph B.,   Daughdrill, Ernest P. Discharged.
Adamson, Charles L.,
Alley, James,   Dodd, John,
Anderson, Walter H.,   Duncan, Walter E.,
Armstrong, James,   Fickett, Albert W., Jr.,
Atkins, Joseph,   Frierson, Leland,
Barnwell, Eugene C.,   George, Bartley T.,
Bentley, William F.,   Glasscock, Jone G.,
Brown, Albert C.,   Graff, Laban C.,
Burgin, Darby,   Gratz, Alexander H.,
Burke, Thomas J.,   Guthrie, William E.,
Campbell, Augustus,   Harris, Albert T.,
Craton, Thomas,   Hatter, Ira S.,
Cook, Theodore A.,   Hambright, Bart H.,
Dann, Peter,   Hannigan, Daniel,
Day, Jack,   Haddock, William,
Day, Frank,   Henderson, William F.,
Daly, Patrick,   Howard, James,

Huffman, Dock E.,
Hurley, Benjamin,
James, Newton T.,
Jones, Morgan,
Keegan, James L.,
Leonard, William O.,
Link, Lewis I.,
Lucas, Thomas,
Mayne, John F.,
Meadows, Marion W.,
Morris, Elgin W.,
Morris, Alonzo W.,
Morris, William E.,
Oates, John A.,
Odell, James T.,
O'Sullivan, Eugene J.,
Owen, Walter D.,
Paschall, Edward A.,
Pearson, James P.,
Powell, Edwin B.,

Ratliff, Orange S.,
Roberts, Thomas,
Saulsbury, Lennard L.,
Schley, Leonard P.,
Sharrit, Amos L.,
Seawright, Jack C.,
Simpson, Edward,
Skinner, Edwin R.,
Sparks, William E.,
Stribling, Lyman F.,
Suttle, David,
Stone, James II.,
Titus, Frank E.,
Tippler, Benjamin F.,
Tucker, Larkin S.,
Webb, Geo. B.,
Williams, John L.,
Williams, Richard L.,
Williams, John II.,
Zuber, Lee K.,

DISCHARGED.

Johnson, Henry L.,
Ross, Edward A.,
Russell, Gilbert E.,
Baggett, Jesse A. Physical disability.
Davidson, George B. Physical disability.

TRANSFERRED.

Fore, Rufus B. To hospital corps.
Wadsworth, Lewis D. To hospital corps.
Dinning, Joseph. To Co. C.
Jones, John H. To Co. C.
Mack, William. To Co. C.

Hengl, Joseph L. To Co. G.
Noble, Charles O. To regimental band.

DIED.

McCullough, Robert J. At Marion hospital, Mobile, Ala., June 27, 1898. Buried in National cemetery, Mobile, June 28, 1898.

DESERTERS.

Jordan, Zack G. July 14, 1898.
Brown, James P. July 23, '98.
Hood, Joseph F. August 4, '98.
Kleiber, John L. Aug. 17, '98.

To Robert W. Huey was chiefly due the credit for Company L's organization. At first, the command was a detachment of the Birmingham Rifles but on July 21, 1893, it was mustered into the state service as Company L of the

Second Regiment, A. N. G., becoming widely known by the name of its organizer. In the military reorganization that subsequently occurred, the command was shifted into the Third Regiment, though continuing to be designated by its original company letter.

At East Lake, in 1894, the Huey Guards rendered valuable service in repressing the coal miners' and American Railway Union riots of that year. Captain Hart, since numbered with the departed martyrs, was in command. At the time of the company's inception, in 1893, he was serving as first sergeant of the Birmingham Rifles and the Huey Guards, without solicitation on his part, called him to their first lieutenancy. He had held a commission in the Minnesota National Guard and was therefore fitted to succeed to the captaincy of the Huey Guards.

In April, 1898, before the president had issued his call for volunteers, Lieutenant N. D. Lacy, then in command of the company, called the members together. He set forth the imminence of war with Spain and asked the militiamen to express their wishes concerning active service. A majority favored an immediate tender of the company to the governor. Accordingly, Lieutenant Lacy telegraphed Governor Johnston and received in response a message announcing that Colonel Higdon had been instructed with relation to his regiment's services. Thus, the Huey Guards claim the honor of being the first company in Alabama that offered its services to the nation in the Spanish-American war.

Meanwhile, Captain Hart, who had resigned his commission in order to engage in business at Jacksonville, Fla., hastened to Alabama to fight with his militia comrades. He was chosen to lead the company and was mustered in as its captain. After his death, at Jacksonville, First Lieutentant Lacy was elected to the captaincy, the second lieutenant being promoted one step. First Sergeant George R. Byrum and Sergeant John S. Hargrove competed for the second lieutenancy and though the latter secured a plurality of the company's votes, the former was commissioned because of his eminent fitness for the position.

COMPANY A.
Woodlawn Light Infantry.

WILLIAM JAY PARKES, Captain.

MORGAN FELIX WOOD, 1st Lieut.
(Appointed Regimental Quartermaster Sept. 5, 1898.)

WILLIAM MUDD MARTIN, 1st Lieut.   LUCIEN C. MONTGOMERY, 2d Lieut.

Sergeants:

Alfred W. Baker, First Sergeant.   Ellie W. Bullock, Q. M. Sergt.
Garland Kirvan,   Arthur W. McDaniel,
V. Walter Smith (Died July 15, 1898). Mack Rittenberry.
Alonzo H. Abel,.

Corporals:

J. Haywood Bullock,   William F. Young,
Louis J. Blau,   John W. Vendrick.
Shannon Jones,   Thomas E. Greene,
Walker J. McCarty,   Samuel I. Bingham.

William T. Lyons, Musician.
Richard R. McFarlin, Artificer.   Riley S. Dorough, Wagoner.

Privates:

Arvin, William H.,
Anderson, Fred,
Alexander, Joseph F.,
Bare, William G.,
Beckley, Orange T.,
Bowers, Alonzo F.,
Barnes, George L. Discharged Sept. 12, 1898.
Buchanan Harry M.,
Cooper, John O.,
Cooper, W. E.,
Connelly, John,
Cox, Sidney L.,
Creiley, Otto C.,
Cunningham, William J.,
Daniel, Earl P.,
Draper, Lewis A. Discharged Sept. 7, 1898.
Dubose, James A.,
Dupey, W. L. Transferred to Co. C.
Dwyer, John.,
Ferrie, Jacob T.,
Frazer, James A.,
Geis, Arthur I.,
Graham, J. Waller,
Honn, Hermann,
Hunt, Frank E.,
Hambright, Pate H.,
Hanesberger, G. C. Transferred to Co. C.
Hazelwood, James,
Holt, Thomas E.,
Johnson, Pearce M.,
Jones, Calvin M.,
Keirsey, David B.,
Lawler, Charles A.,
Landrum, Houston D.,

Lee, Pat J.,
Lee, George F.,
Lee, Frank G.,
McCombs, Charles,
McCombs, J. Wallace,
McIntosh, Robert,
McBurney, Harry J.,
Maloney, Frank J.,
Marsden, Isaac,
Middleton, James,
Marble, Allister E. Transferred to Co. C.
Montgomery, Bert,
Montgomery, George H ,
Moran, Thomas A.,
Noland, James P.,
Norman, James E.,
Norton, Thomas S.
Nail, William F.,
Nunn, William M.,
O'Connell, William S.,
Osger, Frank,
Phillips, William C.,
Powell, Frank C.,
Parrett, G. Frank,
Quirouet, William E ,
Reed, James,
Reed, John,
Reese, William,
Rock, Thomas J.,
Ruddrick, John F.,
Stanley, Arthur L.,
Stirling, Charles T.,
Scroggins, Jerry M.,
Stewart, George W.,
Stewart, James M. Died Aug. 23, 1898.
Smith, Albert,
Smith, John E. Bandman.
Smith, John F.,
Smith, Charles W.,
Small, George E.,
Stowe, Fred S. Bandman.
Tate, Porter K.,
Tyler, Charles A.,
Tyler, William,
Vann, Hobert H. Discharged Sept. 12, 1898.
Veitch, Gideon W.,
Walsh, Patrick H.,
Wells, William,
Welsh, Michael J.,
Williams, Byron L. Company Clerk.
Wims, Martin E.
Wood, Walker F. Discharged Sept. 9, 1898.
Wright, Mark A.,
Yingling, David C.,
Zaner, I. Benton.

Charles W. Grace, musician, discharged Aug. 31, 1898.
Maurice D. Marble, musician, transferred to Co. C.

To the people of Woodlawn, Ala., the Woodlawn Light Infantry has been ever since its organization a sacred institution. The diligence with which the company constantly sought to perfect itself lent credit to the town whose name it bore ; and wherever the command was summoned it took with it the best wishes and hopes of Woodlawn. The Light Infantry's militia record was of the brightest character ; and that the company was among the first to reach the state rendezvous on May 1, 1898, occasioned no surprise.

The Woodlawn Light Infantry, as Company A, Third Regiment, A. N. G., was offered to the governor for service in the volunteer army before the regular call for state troops was issued. The company reported for duty with a relatively large roster of available men. But the surgeons rejected the commander, Captain Parkes. His militia service, however, had shown so many desirable qualifications that influence was brought to bear at Washington to overcome the examining surgeons' objections. Captain Parkes previously commanded the Capital City Guards, of Atlanta, Ga. The Woodlawn Light Infantry were indisposed to relinquish him for another leader and the company was for awhile in an unusually unpleasant dilemma. The First Battalion of the First Alabama was to have been mustered, May 9, but the Woodlawn company declined to take the oath until assured that Capt. W. J. Parkes would lead them. Captain Parkes was much chagrined at the action of his men and told them he feared their course would appear to have been influenced by him. He made the men a talk on the matter, urging them to be mustered. They were firm, however, saying they would follow Captain Parkes to the end of the earth; if the government did not want their commander the government did not want the Woodlawn Light Infantry. So only Companies K, L and G were mustered May 9. The following day, however, word came from Washington authorizing Captain Parkes' acceptance and his company took the oath of service at 9 a. m.

The company served through the Spanish-American war without untoward incident, maintaining its accustomed standard of soldierliness. At Camp Cuba Libre, First Lieut. Morgan Felix Wood was appointed regimental quartermaster and Second Lieut. Will Mudd Martin succeeded him as the company's first lieutenant. Sergeant Lucien C. Montgomery was then chosen second lieutenant.

COMPANY G.

Jefferson Volunteers. (Birmingham, Ala.)

HUGHES B. KENNEDY, Captain.

RICHARD B. GOING, 1st Lieut.   F. E. DAVIDSON, 2d Lieut.

Sergeants:

L. F. Luckie, First Sergeant.   Fred B. Kelso, Q'master Sergeant.
L. S. Hanley, Jr.,   J. Cary Thompson,
C. T. Thomason,   W. Frank King.

Corporals:

Fred W. Bowron,   A. Newman Farley,
J. Emmett Benton,   William C. Perkins,
James G. Johns,   Berlin R. Starnes,
John G. Cobb,   Wallace Smith.

Robt. L. Gregory.
Charles W. Manley, Musician.
Ernest L. Weiss, Cook.   Robert L. Daniels, Artificer.
Thos. Smith, Wagoner.

Privates:

Alfred, Charles A.,   Eastman, P. M.,
Baxter, Robert,   Fancher, Julian L.
Bracknell, Albert,   Fillingen, Barney,
Bean, Alex. W.,   Fletcher, Frank,
Burton, William L.,   Gilbert, Albert,
Bragdon, ——   Gettins, Pat,
Brown, Lewis,   Goodman, Melvin,
Brown, Walter,   Gorman, A. A.,
Boyd, Charles.   Harris, Houston,
Bean, Aelx. W.,   Harris, S.,
Creasy, Burtis E.,   Hend, Eugene F.,
Carson, Albert D.,   Hayes, Charles,
Carson, Clarence E.,   Hunter, John R.,
Coleman, Tillman,   Hengl, Jos. L.,
Caffee, Robert H.,   Hosmer, Van,
Cunningham, Modie E.,   Johnson, A Syd,
Duke, James B.,   Jennings, Charles D.,
Dee, Leslie,   Jones, Ernest,
Daly, Martin W.,   Joller, Edgar R.,
Evans, Frank A.,   Kimball, John C.,
Ellis, Clarence B.,   Kimball, Robin C.,

Keiling, Harry,
Lawley, Fred B.,
Lewis, Herbert,
Levy, Julius,
Mackey, Ed C., Jr.,
Magness, John,
Martin, Tom A.,
Martin, James,
Meagher, James,
Nelson, W. Jones,
Norwood, William W.,
O'Hear, Arthur,
O'Rear, Jas A.,
Pierce, ——,
Pitts, G. Chapman,
Pickard, Toney,
Reeves, Walter,
Russell, John,
Rice, Charles E.,
Ray, Charles E.,
Summers, R. Fletcher,
Shaw, William,
Shaw, Orish W.,
Schwend, Frederick W.,
Stephens, John,
Schilling, Frank,
Short, Malcolm C.,
Tutwiler, J. Cooke,
Tutwiler, Tom,
Venelle, Edward C.,
Walthall, Hay B.,
Wallace, Pulaski,
Witte, Hermon,
White, Thomas W.,
Winters, Jonathan,
Winston, Edward C., Jr.,
Wooley, David C.,
Yancey, William L.

DISCHARGED.

Browne, George M.,
Browne, Richard,
Gregory, Robert L.,
Kline, Ahl,
Vaughn, Harris C.,
LaPointe, Ernest,
Swanson, A. Gulmer,
Steele, James G.,
Vickers, James, Jr.,

DIED.

Finch, Sergeant Philip Neeley.

No company in the First Alabama ranked higher on drill than the Jefferson Volunteers. Organized in 1888 as a zouave company, the "J. V's" never failed to distinguish themselves at every encampment they attended. Louis V. Clark was the company's first captain. Under the efficient command of Captain Clark, who afterward became brigadier general of the state militia, the company was readily recognized as a crack zouave team. Afterward, however, the Jefferson Volunteers became a regular infantry company. After several reorganizations, it was finally captained by H. B. Kennedy, who resigned in 1892. He was succeeded by First Lieut. John K. Warren. The latter resigned in 1896 to accept an appointment on the staff of Brigadier General

Clark. Then Captain Kennedy was recalled to the company's command.

When the call for volunteers came in April, 1898, no militia organization in Alabama evinced more patriotic enthusiasm than did the Jefferson Volunteers. Indeed, it was afterward a company boast that no other command in the state reported at Mobile with a larger percentage of old members. Forty of the company's national guardsmen went with Captain Kennedy to Camp Clark. First Lieut. C. H. Schoolar did not volunteer with his company, however, and on the train, en route to Mobile, May 1, 1893, it was decided that Second Lieutenant Going should be elevated to the first lieutenancy. Then, after a spirited contest, Second Sergt. O. J. Miles was chosen second lieutenant over Sergeants Davidson and Luckie. Lieutenant Miles, however, was afterward rejected by the examining surgeons. Meanwhile, Sergeant Davidson was detailed as special instructor of the guard at Camp Clark. After Lieutenant Miles was rejected, Sergeant Davidson was finally elected second lieutenant.

Death struck a shining mark in Company G—Sergt. Philip Neeley Finch, a son of Mrs. Julia Neeley Finch, the authoress. He died at the division hospital at Jacksonville from typhoid fever contracted in Miami.

It would be difficult to speak too highly of the Jefferson Volunteers' record as a company in the volunteer army. But in fairness it can be said that no other command in the two Alabama regiments excelled it in point of military proficiency.

COMPANY II.

Bessemer Rifles.

THOMAS T. HUEY, Captain.
JAMES B. HOUSTON, 1st. Lieut.   JAMES M. PERKINS, 2d. Lieut.

Sergeants:

Louis N. Mullen, First Sergeant.   Nick L. Nail, Q'master Sergeant.
Wm. Edwards,   Grey J. Huffman,
Joe H. Wiles,   Gus A. Hagan.

Corporals:

C. E. Falkner,   Hugo Robbins,
Joe T. Crawford,   Joe F. Hines,
Ed A. Linch,   John Reilly.
Frank Lyons,

Charles Seay and Paul Copeland, Musicians.
A. H. H. Poppe, Artificer.   Thos. L. Saxon, Wagoner.

Privates:

Adams, Ed.,   Fuls, Adolph,
Allbright, Z. B.,   Gary, Thos.,
Annesley, Jack,   Gentry, Jas. H.,
Ayers, Robert L.,   Gerst, Chas.,
Babcock, Wirt A.,   Gibb, John,
Balcomb, W. W.,   Gladden, Jack,
Baxley, Benj. F.,   Goocher, Joe.,
Bethea, J. F.,   Graham, Miner E.,
Blankenship, Richard, Gurney, J. Frank,
Blevins, Chas. H.,   Hale, George,
Bond, Wm.,   Hardwick, Chas. P.
Bullard, Geo.,   Harry, Lawrence,
Cadenhead, W. A.,   Hoster, Adolph E.
Cates, Chas.,   Houston, Geo.,
Camp, Jas. H.,   Howard, Edw. G.,
Cole, Wm. R.,   Hyland, Dennis J.
Curren, John,   Kelly, W. Edw.,
Craig, Abe,   Kelly, John,
Davidson, John,   Knapp, Anton,
Donnell, T. John,   Kobler, James F.,
Edmonson, L. E.,   Lipscomb, J. A.,
Edmonson, Joe,   Mahone, Wm. L.,
Edwards, C. B.,   Marbut, Harry I.,
Fuhrman, J. F.,   Martin, Arthur M.,

Miller, Joel,
Miller, Dave,
Moran, Thos. W.,
Motley, Jas. H.,
Mullins, Wm. D.,
Norris, J. C.,
Norris, M. Luther,
Nunnally, Wm. G.,
Parsons, Ira,
Pinkerton, Chas.,
Pendley, J. J.,
Polk, Dave A.,
Raybon, George,
Ragsdale, Eugene,
Reeves, E. A.,
Reeves, T. O.,
Robertson, John,
Robertson, Robert L.,
Russell, John C.,
Salter, John D.,
Sapp, Ben. R.,
Schaffer, Albert,
Sexton, Wm. E.,
Simmons, R. L.,
Simmons, W. S. H.,
Smith, E. C.,
Smith, Lawrence,
Spain, F. J.,
Taylor, O. H.,
Thomas, Henry,
Tragesser, Fred. C.,
Tremholm, C. V.,
Tussie, D. C.,
Waller, E. L.,
Weed, J. Walter,
Westberg, Knute,
Williams, W. Lon,
Wilson, C. C.,
Witherspoon, Hugh,
Zolleycoffer, Jas. W.

Company H was organized in Bessemer, Ala., on April 12, 1890, by T. J. Cornwell, a prominent business man. He served two years as captain and was succeeded by Thomas M. Owens, a lawyer and son-in-law of Congressman Bankhead. Captain Owens, who made a most efficient officer, resigned to accept a federal position. His successor, George D. Waller, "rose from the ranks." In June, 1894, he commanded his company at Ensley, Ala., with the result that no organization in the state won more laurels during the labor troubles of that year than did the Bessemer Rifles.

Captain Waller resigned to study medicine, leaving Alabama for that purpose. The "war captain," Thomas T. Huey, who succeeded him, was no less popular than his predecessors. Captain Huey was city treasurer of Bessemer when the national call to arms came. He relinquished a charming home and excellent civic prospects to lead his company.

In Company H, military competence was common. All the company's commanders, save the first, worked their way up from the ranks; and among the "non-coms" were men who had at different times demonstrated their fitness to command companies. One of these, Sergeant Gus Hagan, served for a time in the national guard as first lieutenant of the Lomax Rifles, of Mobile.

COMPANY D.

Anniston Rifles (Regimental Color Company).

GEO. W. TUMLIN, Captain.

BRENTON R. FIELD, 1st Lieut.   HAMILTON BOWIE, 2d Lieut.

Sergeants:

C. W. Sproull, First Sergeant.
James B. Garrison,
Charles H. Jackson,
Jas. A. Wilkerson, Q'm'ter Sergt.
Chas. A. Wilkerson,
A. N. McLeod, Color Sergeant.

Corporals:

S. F. Cornelius,
Sam Noble,
F. W. Beasley,
Howard S. Williams,
J. J. Gladden,
Fred H. Roussaville,
B. W. Ingersoll,

George Worth, Chas. Herron, Hance Hall, Musicians.
Burke Hanford, Artificer.   J. P. Hale, Wagoner.
Frank Rohner, Mascot.

Privates:

Arberry, Wakefield. Transferred to Hospital Corps.
Adams, Wm. H.,
Amrin, Wm.,
Brown, W. E.,
Banks, Walter,
Bates, Clanton,
Benford, Benjamin,
Blake, Asa,
Boguski, Wm,
Bowman, W. D.,
Black, R. C.,
Branch, Henry,
Burge, James,
Burns, Ben E.,
Burns, John F.,
Breadion, Wm.,
Carter, Thos.,
Cary, Edgar,
Comeaux, W. E.,
Cook, Wm.,
Costner, Alfred,
Conyers, E. L.,
Coulter, N. H.,
De Loney, O. T.,
Evans, W. G.,
Emberg, Oscar,
Fancher, Eugene,
Freeman, Ernest,
Flynn, Owen,
Frederick, Wm.,
Futrell, G. W.,
Gilbert, Lon,
Goff, J. W.,
Griffin, Luther,
Gunn, Elwood,
Guill, Reuben,
Goeddel, J. Albert,
Hall, R. E.,
Hall, Leo. J.,
Hampton, John S.,
Hutchens, Henry,
Head, Joe,
Hogan, R. J.,

Herz, Carl,
Inman, Jas. B.,
Jackson, Sydney,
Jackson, W. F.,
Johnson, Columbus,
Kopp, Fred,
Killough, W. S.,
Land, H. W.,
Lane, Wynatt,
Layton, Chas.,
Learned, W. L.,
Lloyd, S. C.,
McDonald, Jas. D,
McRae, Harrison,
McGowan, W. W.,
McMillen, LaFayette,
Mordue, Robert,
Moore, E. H,
Minor, S. D.,
Nabers, French,
Purdy, Bradley,
Randolph, Arthur.
Rogers, J. W.,
Reeves, Wm.,
Ritch, A. E..
Ryan, Patrick,
Reynolds, Wm.,
Salmon, Newman,
Sansom, Collier,
Sellers, W. D.,
Smith, Richard,
Samples, H. S.,
Schmitt, Theo.,
Skudlas, Andrew,
Sutton, J. W.,
Tally, J. W.,
Tensley, Oakley,
Thomas, Chas.,
Turner, Lon,
Turner, Jake,
Vann, D. Paul. Transferred to Hospital Corps.
Watson, Chas. P.,
Watts, John T.,
Williams, Tom,
Williams, Tom G.,
Williams, W. H.,
Westbrook, M. C.,
Whisenant, R. G.,
Young, John W.,
Yongue, Willie. Discharged.

The Anniston Rifles were among the first companies to report for duty at Camp Clark. The command's creditable record in the state militia was sustained in the volunteer army. Indeed, Company D was one of those companies from which little was heard save when need of their services arose. Then, the entire command met the emergency as one man.

Company D's position as the right center company of the Second Battalion entitled it to the colors, A. N. McLeod being appointed the color sergeant before Camp Clark was fairly established. The company reached Mobile, May 1, and was mustered in May 13.

CAPT. NEWMAN D. LACY,
CO. L, FIRST REGIMENT ALA. VOLS.

COMPANY M.

Clark Rifles (Pratt City and Talladega).

ROMAINE BOYD, Captain.

THOMAS HARDEMAN, 1st Lieut.   R. G. MALLETT, 2d Lieut.

Sergeants:

H. S. Meade, First Sergeant.   D. P. Armstrong, Q'master Sgt.
C. L. Cansler,   Peter Meehl.
Jack Fallon,   Charles Caldwell.

Corporals:

John B. Askew,   Z. W. Grogan,
F. A. Meier,   Hugh Montgomery,
J. C. Scarbrough,   Isaac B. Price.

Fred. Raper, Musician.
Z. B. Bonner, Artificer.   E. B. Costner, Wagoner.

Privates:

Atchison, L.,   Harvill, L. B.,
Ballard, G. W.,   Haun, John W.,
Barnhill, G. R.,   Henderson, E.,
Bergin, John D.,   Hobbs, M. D.,
Biddington, S.,   Hyde, H.,
Bowie, Leroy,   Isbell, Thos. L.,
Braden, Wm. B.,   Kelly, Mike,
Brame, Jas. E.,   Langford, Wm. H.,
Brewer, E. A.,   Lemon, H. H.,
Burkholder, C. F.,   Leonard, Ernest,
Callahan, F. A.,   Lewis, Edward,
Davidson, D.,   Lynn, Earnest,
Davis, Thos. G.,   Martin, Landy,
Davis, W. G.,   Martin, Ed.,
Delp, Grant,   Mason, Dick,
Durrett, James,   McCann, M. J.,
Edney, Wm. A.,   McClung, D. D.,
Fancher, R. M.,   Milam, W. H.,
Fancher, Wm. S.,   Moon, Lonie. Deserted.
Findlay, Joe M.,   Nichols, F.,
Franklin, Wm. M. Dead.   Oliver, J. B.,
Godley, Charles,   Oliver, R. A.,
George, James,   O'Niell, A.,

Palvado, C.,
Parker, M. W.,
Peebles, John T.,
Pennington, N. B.,
Powers, E.,
Putnam, W. D.,
Phillips, E. T.,
Price, Jack,
Prowell, R. A.,
Prowell, Wm. J.,
Reese, Geo. B.,
Reeves, Fred,
Rooks, Robert,
Royster, F. M.,
Scarbrough, J. H.,
Seibert, Adolph,
Sewell, Wm. H.,
Shore, O. G.,
Simpson, Frank,
Sims, Wm. C.,
Slate, John M.,
Smith, Wm.,
Smith, J. S.,
Smithson. T.,
Speer, Samuel J.,
Stack, Hugh,
Stewart, James H.,
Stich, Fred M.,
Sullivan, D.,
Tankersly. D. D.,
Trent, Charles A.,
Turner, John,
Tyson, Claudius,
Vincent, A.,
Ware, B. M.,
Williams, J. L.,
Hodo, Joe M.

H. Brada, committed suicide, July 12, 1898, at Miami, Fla.

On April 26, 1898, just five days after war was declared by the United States and three days after Governor Johnston's call for volunteers, application was made to the state executive for permission to raise a company of eighty men at Pratt City, Ala. But four days remained until the date set for the First Regiment's departure from Birmingham for Mobile. About sixty men had signed papers in Pratt City agreeing to volunteer, but the approach of May 1 rendered them restless and many threatened to join other companies unless their own command was at once completed. At that juncture, General L. V. Clark, who was in close touch with the whole military organization of the state, effected a consolidation between the Pratt City men headed by Thomas Hardeman and E. D. Johnston and a similar body from Talladega under Romaine Boyd. It was understood that the Pratt City contingent would name the two lieutenants while the leader of the Talladega element was to become captain. Before the muster, however, E. D. Johnston was named regimental adjutant and R. G. Mallett succeeded him as one of the Pratt City leaders. On May 1, the company left for Mobile, the state rendezvous, Captain Boyd departing from Talladega with thirty-one men and the Pratt City contingent leaving Birmingham, thirty strong. The latter party originally numbered forty-three but thirteen of them were lost in the immense throngs that crowded the depot at Birmingham. Nine of those left behind followed afterward, however, through the instrumentality of A. J. Reilly, of Pratt City, who had already befriended the company in various ways.

At Mobile, non-commissioned officers were chosen as follows: J. G. Meagher, first sergeant; D. D. McClung, quartermaster sergeant; J. H. Stewart, Tully Smithson and P. W. Gooch, sergeants; Jack Fallon, Peter Meehl, Dick Mason and John B. Askew, corporals; Z. B. Bonner, artificer; E. B. Costner, wagoner; and Fred Raper, musician.

When the company was finally assigned to its position in the regiment it was decided to adopt the name "Bowie Volunteers," in honor of Mr. Sid Bowie, who spent considerable time and money in aiding the organization. But the state press insisted on crediting General L. V. Clark with the company and dubbed the command "Clark Rifles." This name clung to the company throughout its service.

Changes were made in the non-commissioned personnel by reason of physical rejections and disabilities incurred in camp life. But the commissioned officers remained the same despite an unpleasant campaign that was conducted by a clique against the captain. This coterie's disaffection became so marked and tangible at Camp Cuba Libre that a round robin secured numerous signatures requesting that a board of inquiry be selected to investigate certain charges. This board had successive sittings but the order directing the regiment's muster out was announced before the matter reached a finality.

Company M's organization was the cause of a spirited newspaper controversy between R. C. McFarland, ex-captain of Company B, and Governor Johnston. McFarland had requested permission to raise a company in Lauderdale County, but when failure stared him in the face he consented to a coalition with Captain Boyd, yielding to the latter the captaincy. Afterward, however, it was asserted that he had misrepresented the number of his followers and the company's first lieutenancy was given to Hardeman. Then Lieutenant Mallett's claims were presented for the second lieutenancy and when McFarland found himself "frozen out," he left Camp Clark in high dudgeon. A few days later he was fatally wounded in a primary election brawl in the courthouse at Florence.

COMPANY I.

Oxford Rifles.

ARTHUR HARRISON, Captain.

TOM B. COOPER, 1st. Lieut.   CLIFTON L. SITTON, 2d. Lieut.

Sergeants:

Jas. M. Armstrong, First Sergeant.   Ross Green, Q'master Sergeant.
O. Augustus Hilton,   D. Houston Smith,
David W. Shuford,   Joseph J. Taylor.

Corporals:

John M. Davis,   George Thomas,
Joseph V. Mallory,   Joseph A. Hardin,
David Smyth,   Chas. P. Nunnally, transferred to hospital corps, June 18.
Lewis Postell,
Hampton Draper,

Wm. J. Dodge and Wm. H. Horton, Musicians.
Wm. J. Austin, Artificer.   John A. Barker, Wagoner.

Privates:

Allison, Joshua,   Fulton, Ezekiel,
Austin, Alonzo,   Fulbright, Rufus J.,
Brewton, Jas.,   Fox, Mike,
Bass, Wm.,   Gaines, Nicholas P. Died June 7.
Brown, Lonnie,   Greer, Wm. R.,
Beddoe, George,   Glover, Willis B.,
Bush, George R.,   Gentry, Walter,
Carr, Toney,   Gilmore, Wm.,
Cotney, John J,   Graves, Joseph A.,
Cotney, Ferrell,   Hallifield, Willie,
Crow, Jas. R.,   Harris, Frank. Transferred to hospital corps.
Chambers, Henry L.,
Carnell, Frank,   Hayden, Thos.,
Couch, Carter,   Hand, Chas. C.,
Casper, Clem A.,   Hamilton, Chas. W.,
Cannon, Samuel P.,   Hewett, Edward,
Driver, Archie R.,   Heuse, Ed.,
Dunlap, Charlie,   Hogue, Thos.,
Feminear, Joseph L.,   Horton, Jesse D.,
Fortner, Wm. T,   Johnson, John,
Franklin, Wm. J.,   Johnson, Ernest S.,

Jeffers, Robert H. Deserted Aug. 7.
Jones, John L.,
Jones, Thos.,
Justice, Luther,
Kenneybrook, David,
Lewis, Jas. S.,
Larsen, Norender,
Lott, Jesse G.,
McClurkin, Wm. T.,
Meagher, Wm. P.,
Mallory, David M.,
Mason, Ellod L.,
McCullis, Burrell,
McMillan, Luke H.,
Merritt, Clifford S ,
McConnell, Reuben D.,
Mims, Jas. W.,
McGorman, John,
Nichols, Chas. D.,
Olsen, Olen J. Died June 9.
Phillips, Robert W.,
Ponder, John J.,
Posey, Ambrose P.,
Roberson, Randall R ,
Ray, Ernest P.,
Reynolds, Frank D.,
Shipper, Jas. L.,
Stockdale, Colin,
Sullivan, Richard O.,
Steele, Wm.,
Smith, Edgar D.,
Sorrell, Thos. G.,
Sanders, Jas. P. Deserted June 7.
Shirley, Ed.,
Smith, Allen,
Setliff, Wm. A. Discharged August 5.
Thomas, Frank M.,
Tigett, Charley R.,
Tigett, Porter,
Tice, Wm. G.,
Thompson, William. Died Sept. 21.
Werner, Frank,
Womack, Chas. A.,
Wedgeworth, Wm. A.,
Wood, Wm. M. Discharged Aug. 5.
White, Elijah F.,
Williams, Claude H.,
Yoe, P. G.,
Yeatman, John F.

The company designated as the Calhoun Rifles in the Alabama National Guard came to be known as the Oxford Rifles in the volunteer army. This was largely because the soldiers in the patriot army were inclined to mention companies by the names of the towns from which a majority of the members hailed. Company I was composed of an earnest set of men who sought from the outset to familiarize themselves with the duties and tasks of active campaigning. And the success that attended their efforts was best shown by the satisfaction that the men gave as a command.

The Calhoun or Oxford Rifles reached Camp Clark on May 1 and were mustered in May 14, 1898.

SOUTHERN MARTYRS.

COMPANY C.

Etowah Rifles. (Gadsden, Ala.)

NELSON G. CANNING, Captain.

JOSEPH L. DANIEL, 1st Lieut.   WILLIAM A. HASSON, 2d Lieut.

Sergeants:

William A. Echols, 1st Sergeant.
Wm. P. Gwin,
Earl Lay,
Wm. U. Daughdrill, Q'master Sgt.
Louis W. Pope,
Thos. McHan.

Corporals:

Wm. E. Hughes,
John D. Daughdrill,
Chas. O. Duncan,
Edgar G. Allison,
Edwin B. Slack,
Chas. O. Watt.

Edward M. Standifer and Jesse Turrentine, Musicians.
Ira R. Foster, Company Clerk.   Hubbard L. Hodge, Artificer.
Boyd Hamlin, Wagoner.

Privates:

Arteberry, Jas. R.,
Acker, Peter D.,
Anderson, John C.,
Addington, Augustus,
Abney, Luke L.,
Boalch, George R.,
Burns, Henry R.,
Bain, Robt.,
Burton, Samuel,
Beard, Elli B.,
Boyle, Roddy,
Bilbe, Chas. Transferred to Co. I.
Coleman, Wm.,
Cline, Bob J.,
Caston, Alvah,
Cook, Martin V.,
Collins, John A.,
Chitwood, R. L.,
Durham, John D.,
Davis, Lewis,
Dossett, Wm. L.,
Dinning, Joseph,
Duran, Bub,
Dupuy, Wm. L.,
Dunlap, Robert H.,
Devine, Wm. L.,
Erskine, Walter,
Gardner, Jas. M.,
Gilbreath, Edward W.,
Giles, Dock J.,
Goddard, Wm. S.,
Guined, John B.,
Hill, John W.,
Hannah, J. W. Died.
Hass, Wm. F.,
Horton, Jesse B.,
Hood, Ollie,
Harrison, Henry,
Holland, John W.,
Hinds, James,
Hunter, Jas. L.,

Harbour, John A.,
Harnesberger, G. C., Transferred to Co. B.
Hall, Ed,
Headley, Harry,
Harrelson, W. M.,
Jones, John H.,
Jordan, Albert,
Johnson, Watson C.,
Jones, Wm. J.,
Johnson, Wm. N.,
Keith, Geo. T.,
Lister, Noah E,
Lipscomb, Robt. L.,
Montgomery, Chas. G., Jr. Transferred to Band.
Moore, Lawson L.,
Moore, Jas. F.,
Marble, Maurice D.,
Marble, Alister E.,
McCartney, Mabry,
McMunn, John,
McGrew, Frank M.,
Mackey, Wm. D.,
McNaren, John,
McCurdy, Chas. H.,
McQueen, John R.,
McDonald, Jas.,
Moragne, A. W.,
Mills, John W.,
Mack, Wm. J. Transferred to Band.
Mitchell, Frank B.,
Miller, John E.,
Norris, Chas. F.,
Norman, Rex,
Naugher, Kitrell,
Naugher, Neal J.,
Nix, Calvin,
Paden, John S., Jr.,
Paschall, Florence E. Transferred to Co. B.
Quirk, Edwin A.,
Riley, Walter,
Roberts, Oscar W.,
Richley, Geo. C.,
Rich, Samuel T.,
Rhodes, Jason H.,
Roden, Jas. B.,
Slater, John R.,
Sutton, Stephen D.,
Sibert, Olin W.,
Shatzen, M. L.,
Stallings, Thos.,
Smith, Oliver C.,
Tully, Louis C.,
Willis, Jas. M.,
Wilson, Chas. T.,
Williamee, Robt.,
Young, Reuben,

The Etowah Rifles (Company C) became a national guard organization in 1882, one of the company's lieutenants at that time being H. B. Foster, afterward colonel in the state militia and in May, 1898, appointed senior major of the Second Alabama. In 1886, the Etowah Rifles were ordered to Round Mountain, a mining town, to quell a riot. Again, in 1894, the company aided in the preservation of peace at Ensley City, being commanded at that time by Capt. L. L. Herzberg.

On April 29, 1898, the company, under the command of Capt. Nelson G. Canning, offered itself with fifty-nine enlisted men for service against Spain. The company left Gadsden for Mobile, May 1, 1898, with forty recruits and was mustered in, May 13.

COMPANY E.

Joe Johnston Rifles. (Decatur, Ala.)

WILLIAM E. WALLACE, Captain.

MITCHELL N. PRIDE, 1st. Lieut.   WM. J. WEBB, 2d. Lieut.

Sergeants:

Caesar E. Marks, First Sergeant.   John H. Albes, Q. M. Sergeant.
James W. Joplin,   Philip P. Hawkins,
James H. McCoy,   Graham Banks.

Corporals:

Nelson C. White,   Walter J. Andrews,
Rolston C. Cosby,   James A. McPheeters,
Burton E. Gillespie,   William F. McClary.

Jo H. Carothers and Carl I. Nelson, Musicians.
Peter Borgeson, Artificer.   Miles W. Phillips, Wagoner.

Privates:

Alexander, John R.,
Almon, Dee,
Anderson, Olaus,
Bacon, John E.,
Ballew, William T.,
Banks, Baylor,
Bates, John W.,
Betz, H. Clay.
Black, Charles B.,
Bracken, Martin A.,
Brown, Edgar R.,
Brown, John W.,
Burwell, John T.,
Blanton, Samuel V.,
Carruth, Edwin F.,
Christensen, Henry A.,
Christensen, Myron J.,
Coles, Peter M.,
Cook, Robert W.,
Cooper, John B. Discharged.
Dobbins, John M.,
Drawbaugh, John H.,
Deuring, C. H. F.,
Duke, William R.,
Duncan, Hugh B.,
Ehrensperger, J. J.,
Elmore, Charles H.,
Epperson, John I.,
Golladay, Ottway S. Transferred to Signal Corps.
Harr, Robt. W.,
Hollinger, Perry A.,
Horton, John F. Dead.
Huff, Harry D.,
Hunt, Oscar M.,
Jackson, Jas. L.,
Johnson, Ben J. Jr.,
Jones, John C.,
Keeley, Charles J.,
Kontzen, Noble,
Lamb, Jas. L.,
Lance, James O.,
Lerman, Isaac,
Lewis, John H.,
Lucas, Charles C.,
Martin, Charles J.,

Meacher, George W.,
Myers, Ellsworth,
McBee, Henry B.,
McCormick, Robert B.,
McNew, Frank B.,
Neaves, John H.,
Neaves, William,
Neely, Philip T.,
Norris, Lucien B.,
O'Leary, Arthur,
O'Neil, George W.,
Plemons, Horace N.
Powers, John D.,
Ragsdale, George W.,
Raney, Harry,
Richard, John H.,
Rich, James B.   Discharged.
Roberts, John F.,
Robinson, John C.,
Russell, Ben F.,
Russell, Bert,
Ross, Mitchell A.,
Samples, James E.,
Simms, William H.,
Shindlebower, Charles C.,
Stanley, John E.,
Story, Claude E.,
Sturdivant, Robert L,
Suckfull, George A.,
Terry, John T.,
Thieman, Edward R.,
Tingle, George S.,
Todd, Robert A.,
Tripp, Henry,
Uehlein, William B.,
Unphrey, John D.,
Walker, John W.,
Watson, Sandy G.,
Wynn, John W.

The Joe Johnston Rifles (Company E) assumed their name in the martial spirit that prompted the company's organization. All through the April weeks in which the war horizon grew darker and darker, William E. Wallace was urging the young men of Decatur to "be up and doing." Finally, a meeting was held on the evening of April 29, 1898. Already hostilities had been declared, and the yeomanry and chivalry of Decatur were burning with patriotic ardor. At 9 p. m. it was declared that an organization had been consummated, and Captain O. Kyle was authorized to telegraph to the governor the company's anxiety to fight. An hour and a half later an answer was received accepting the company's services. On May 1, the Joe Johnston Rifles, seventy-six strong, arrived in Mobile.

The company was mustered into the volunteer service on May 13, 1898. But Captain Kyle having been appointed major of the Third Battalion, First Lieutenant W. E. Wallace was made captain; Second Lieutenant M. N. Pride, elevated to first lieutenant, and First Sergeant W. J. Webb elected as second lieutenant.

June 13, 1898, the Joe Johnston Rifles were the centre of a very pretty flag presentation ceremony, Miss Mamie Wallace, the then nine-year-old daughter of Captain Wallace, presenting to the company, in touching words, a handsome banner given by the people of the two Decaturs.

COMPANY F.
Huntsville Rifles.

H. C. LAUGHLIN, Captain.

ROBERT SEARCY DEMENT, 1st Lieut.   T. M. HOOPER, 2d Lieut.

Sergeants:

J. L. Winston, First Sergeant.
Marvin McCary,
J. C. McDonald,
Hyram Burrow, Q'master Sergt.
Chas. M. Ford,
Chas. F. Snyder.

Corporals:

Jas. H. Mastin,
Herbert McLaurine,
S. M. Stewart, Jr.,
Otto Kullman,
Eugene Binford,
Nat Power,
Geo W. Vogel.

P. M. Sloss, Company Clerk.
Chas. H. Halsey, Jr., and Bernard R. Rudford, Musicians.
Allie F. Hall, Artificer.
J. H. Cunningham, Wagoner.

Privates:

Anderson, W. A. Discharged.
Aday, Willett,
Alexander, Walter,
Allen, W. C.,
Barlow, J. H. Transferred to Hospital Corps.
Bennett, W. G.,
Blakeney, H. W.,
Brock, J. P.,
Brooks, M. C.,
Bryant, M. L.,
Blair, D. L.,
Blunt, Jas. A.,
Buford, R. M.,
Buchanan, O.,
Buchanan, J. E.,
Campbell, Add,
Campbell, Wm.,
Cleveland, L. S.,
Coole, W. A.,
Clark, Wm.,
Cramer, Carl,
Crute, J. P.,
Collett, J O.,
Daniel, K. T.,
Daniel, John W.,
Denton, James E.,
Echoff, Frank,
Floyd, S. H.,
Fletcher, Robt,
Fulgham, Jas. B.,
Fullington, M. B,
Gaines, Victor H.,
Gaines, Ira C.,
Green, Wm. T.,
Herz, Wm. G.,
Hill, Samuel,
Hill, Forest,
Hite, David,
Hughes, Enoch F.,

Helvesson, Laurin,
Jaens, John F.,
Jett, David B.,
Jackson, Rufus F.,
King, Edw. L.,
Lauderdale, Thos.,
Lewis, Frank,
Lowe, John T.,
Lyons, Harry,
Mullens, Winburn,
Moore, Horatio R.,
McMahan, John J.,
Mason, Thos. J.,
Norwood W. R.,
O'Reilly, Geo.,
Pritchard, Roy A.,
Pickard, Wm. F.,
Poe, Sam T.,
Power, Herbert,
Requette, Joseph,
Reynolds, Archie J.,
Roberson, John C.,
Sample, Abner C.,
Schulz, Louis,
Schwenke, August,
Searcy, R. T.,
Shafer, C. C.,
Shafer, W. F.,
Scott, Thos. M.,
Spriggs, J. Allen,
Smith, Houston J.,
Smith, L. H.,
Street, R. E,
Steger, Marion E.,
Stewart, C. A.,
Stewart, C. H.,
Stewart, Joseph,
Taylor, Wm. T.,
Vann, Pat,
West, Albert M.,
Webb, Marshall C.,
Willcut, Sam,
Williams, Mack,
Woodward, John W.,
Worley, Rufus J.,

Twice the name of the Huntsville Rifles was changed. The company was reorganized from the Madison Rifles which made a record in the war of the '60's. After that reorganization, the command was known for years as the Monte Sano Light Guards. Then, when service in the volunteer army came, the name was changed to Huntsville Rifles.

The company reached Camp Clark, May 3, and was mustered in, May 13. Some of the incidents in the company's early volunteer record were recounted in the Mobile *Register* of June 13, 1898, as follows:

"It was learned unofficially yesterday that Capt. R. L. Hay, Company F, has resigned his commission. Captain Hay has had considerable trouble with some of his men since he has been here. It developed that one man in the company, Private F. W. Reed, is insane, and his discharge is now pending. Again, Sergeant Hall of this company was stricken with varioloid and removed to the county pesthouse. His messmates, four sergeants, are now in isolation, and practically all of the company work has devolved on Captain Hay. His men have complained constantly of not getting sufficient rations, although the quartermaster states they were supplied the same as other companies who are faring all right. On one occasion, a large number of the men of Company F refused to do drill duty because they were not properly cared for. They were, of course, placed under arrest. Regimental officers claim that the trouble with the company is mismanagement, and consequently Captain Hay has tendered his resignation, which has been forwarded to the War Department."

After Captain Hay's resignation, the captaincy was filled by First Lieutenant Laughlin's promotion, the second lieutenant becoming first lieutenant and First Sergt. T. M. Hooper being elected second lieutenant.

That the Huntsville Rifles bore with them the best wishes of their home town was evidenced by the handsome banner presented by the people of Huntsville to the company and the substantial cash donations made from time to time to purchase comforts for the command.

COMPANY B.
Wheeler Rifles (Florence, Ala.)

WM. MITCHELL MARTIN, Captain.

ROBT. L. BROWN, 1st Lieut. ROBT. E. SIMPSON, 2d Lieut.

Sergeants:

Robt. M. Martin, First Sergeant. James J. Challen, Q'm'ter Sergt.
H. A. Frantz, S. P. McDonald,
John W. Martin, Price Abernathy.

Corporals:

Andrew Sharp, D. P. Bibb,
Henry J. Moore, W. L. Lawrence,
Jas. A. Burger, Tom E. Sanford,
M. W. Keenan,

H. B. Garrett and John Williams, Musicians.
Andrew Smith, Artificer. N. D. Phillips, Wagoner.

Privates:

Arthur, G. C., Evans, Ed,
Armstead, Gus, Ferguson, J. B.,
Armstead, Ike, Harrison, Green,
Alexander, S. E., Houston, Irvine,
Autry, Elmore, Hindman, Sam C.,
Bernst, O. M., Hipp, Geo. C.,
Brown, Robt., Holden, J. M.,
Bowen, D. V., Hyde, Ike,
Brown, Geo. L., Hendrix, Percy R.,
Burcham, Sam, Horton, D. P.,
Byrd, Bob, Hauerwas, J. C.,
Curry, Jas. F., Julian, Wm. C.,
Crow, J. M., James, Chas.,
Creel, Geo., Johnston, H. M.,
Coyle, Mike, McDaniel, Ollie Thomas
Challen, Frank N., McPeters, A. L.,
Chambliss, Pomroy, Matthews, E. A.,
Castile, Frank, Morrison, J. W.,
Dill, Frank, Morrison, F. O.,
Dean, Lawrence, McDonald, F. M.,
Day, Ed, McKey, R. B.,

McKey, P. L.,
Morgan, B. P.,
Millard, L. M.,
Nichols, J. A.,
Norris, Chas. F.,
Patton, T. D.,
Paulk, J. C.,
Potts, John,
Powers, C. J.,
Pride, Wm. M., Jr.   Dead.
Pride, Joe P.,
Pruett, E. W.,
Pullen, Webb M.,
Pullen, Wm. H.,
Rhodes, W. E.,
Rossen, W. M,
Rogers, F. M.,
Russell, Henry J.,
Scales, Vance,
Simpson, Richard W.,
Sutton, M. M.,
Sherman, W. T.,
Stephenson, W. W.,

Satterfield, E. H.,
Stout, E. C.,
Stafford, John R.,
Sweeten, A. E.,
Seawell, R. F.,
Simmons. Wm. J.,
Schall, Geo.,
Sagely, J. C.,
Tompkins, Ernest,
Thornton, M ,
Walters, Elsie,
Wiggins, Henry,
Wiley, F. F.,
Waters, E. B.,
Weston, J. M.,
Young, J. E.,

DISCHARGED:

McFarland, A., Sergeant,
Lay, B. C.,
Torian, Sam,
Moody, Otis.

Company B, the Wheeler Rifles, came into existence in 1887-88. Julian Field was the first captain. At Birmingham, during the industrial demonstrations and difficulties of 1894, the company was of material service. On three different occasions, the command was called out to guard the county jail at Florence from the violence of mobs which had gathered to lynch prisoners.

Forty of the company's fifty members volunteered their services for the Spanish-American war, and thirty-five of them finally reported for duty at Camp Clark in Mobile. R. C. McFarland, a newspaper man, who met a tragic end in Florence shortly after the company assembled in Mobile, had been captain, but when his commission expired a year before, First Lieutenant Martin was elected to succeed him. Second Lieutenant Brown became the first lieutenant and Corporal Robert E. Simpson was chosen second lieutenant.

MAJ. HENRY B. FOSTER.
COMMDG. FIRST BATTALION, SECOND REGIMENT ALA. VOLS.

This excerpt from a Mobile paper of May 19, 1898, tells matters of interest concerning the company:

"The Wheeler Rifles represent the highest type of North Alabama manhood. William Mitchell Martin, the captain, is the youngest company commander in the state. He is twenty-four years old. He joined the company when sixteen years of age and has been with it continuously since that time. Captain Martin was assistant cashier of the Merchants' Bank of Florence when the call was made for volunteers. He is a son of Robert D. Martin, who was with Forrest's cavalry in the Confederate service. The young commander has a brother, Robert M. Martin, who is first sergeant of the company, who also gave up a lucrative position in a rival bank at Florence. First Lieutenant Robert L. Brown is a prominent young jeweler at Florence, and a son of Andrew Brown, who was with General Wheeler's cavalry in the late war. Second Lieutenant Robert E. Simpson, of the Wheelers, is a young lawyer of Florence, who was reared at Covington, Lauderdale county. His father, Preston Simpson, was also a member of Wheeler's cavalry in the late war. These three officers were tendered commissions in the regular army by General Joe Wheeler upon the declaration of war, but declined the honor in order to serve with the company which they had striven so hard to place upon the high plane it has reached as a military organization."

REGIMENTAL BAND

OF THE

FIRST ALABAMA.

O. WOLFF, Chief Musician.   R. EMMETT CRADDOCK, Drum Major.

George W. Worth,
George L. Brown,
Paul Copeland,
Hance Hall,
Sydney Hecker,
Charles Herron,
William Mack,
John McNulty,
Charles Montgomery,
Charles O Noble,
Wade Rogers,
Forrest A. Chase,
John E. Smith,
Fred S. Stowe,
John P. Terry,
Wyper Menzies.

The First Alabama band's organization was not perfected until the regiment reached Miami. Up to that time, however, competent musicians were being enlisted as they offered themselves, Fred S. Stowe having been detached from the Woodlawn Light Infantry and detailed to look after the bandmen until the musicians were organized.

Colonel Higdon made requisition for the band instruments without delay. He was determined that the regiment should not spend the $400 or $500 necessary to purchase the band-pieces out of its regimental fund. He considered that such an amount of money could be used to better advantage in other ways. For this reason the First Alabama was practically without a band until after the Miami encampment. In the interim, however, every effort was made to have a competent set of musicians on hand to use the instruments when they arrived. The bandmaster was summoned from a distant part of the country and the enlisted bandmen were afforded every possible opportunity to practice on makeshift or borrowed instruments.

August 2, 1898, Colonel Higdon was notified at Miami that the regiment's band instruments had been shipped to him. A few days later word was received that the regiment had been ordered to Porto Rico; and the efforts to perfect the band organization were redoubled. Even after intelligence reached the regiment that it would probably not go to Porto Rico, the bandmaster perseveringly endeavored to bring his band to a high standard of musical proficiency.

In view of the many discouraging circumstances that arose, it is only fair to say that the First Alabama band made better progress and accomplished better results than could have been reasonably expected of it. Indeed, before the muster out, the band was able to furnish very entertaining music and at Jacksonville it was one of the best features of the regimental dress parades.

SECOND REGIMENT ALABAMA VOLUNTEER INFANTRY.

JAMES WADE COX, Colonel Commanding.
WALTER A. THURSTON, Lieutenant Colonel.

MAJORS:
    First Battalion,   HENRY B. FOSTER.
    Second Battalion,   ROBERT B. Du MONT.
    Third Battalion,   WILLIAM W. BRANDON.

SURGEONS:
    Major,   S. S. PUGH.
    First Lieutenant,   JAMES N. McLAIN.
    First Lieutenant,   WALTER R. WEEDON.

CHAPLAIN:
    Captain,   A. C. HARTE.

REGIMENTAL ADJUTANT:
    First Lieutenant,   JOHN R. VIDMER.

REGIMENTAL QUARTERMASTER:
    First Lieutenant,   WILLIAM E. MICKLE, Jr.

BATTALION ADJUTANTS:
    (First Lieutenants)
    First Battalion,   C. C. HARE.
    Second Battalion,   SHERWOOD BONNER.
    Third Battalion,   WILLIAM Y. JOHNSTON.

NON-COMMISSIONED STAFF:
    Sergeant Major,   E. THURSTON BONHAM.
    Quartermaster Sergeant,   CHARLES B. TOWNSEND.
    Hospital Stewards, W. A. LYTLE, COBB NICHOLS and F. L. HURT.

MEN OF THE SECOND ALABAMA.

COMPANY A.
Montgomery Greys.

HERBERT B. MAY, Captain.

JAMES H. MCTYEIRE, 1st. Lieut.   JACOB T. BULLEN, 2nd. Lieut.

Sergeants:

Harry C. Carter, First Sergeant.   Joseph G. King, Q'master Sergt.
Dudley C. Williamson,   John G. Williamson,
Berto H. Johnson,   David W. Crosland.

Robert F. Rohan, Chief Trumpeter.

Corporals:

Walter M. Eckford,   Lawrence V. Calhoun,
Kerney W. McDade,   Elwood J. Pearson,
Robert K. Blackshear,   Harry L. Trowbridge.

John A. Lord, Musician.

Joseph R. Williams, Artificer.   John A. Oliver, Wagoner.

Privates:

Barron, Wallace S.,   Davis, Thomas W.,
Bonham, Olin F.,   Ennis, William H.,
Baker, William D.,   Gartman, Eugene L.,
Brown, Asa W.,   Gingles, Harvey M.,
Buttimer, Daniel J.,   Grider, John D.,
Baxley, William H.,   Goodman, Clem,
Blackburn, Sam M.,   Guy, William J.,
Bartlett, Robert L.,   Harmon, John L.,
Brackin, Ras L.,   Hillman, Hudson,
Bingham, William H.,   Higgins, Bert,
Carmichael, Malcom S.,   Holt, John B.,
Cardon, Jacob L.,   Holt, Bolling H.,
Chapman, George T.,   Howard, Benjamin,
Cloud, James T.,   Hammond, Ab. G.,
Clair, Earl W.,   Ham, Jesse M.,
Drae, Robert L.,   Hildbrand, John,

Jones, Thomas,
Jones, George W.,
Jones, William T.,
Jones, Joseph A.,
Judkins, Joseph H.,
Lee, John D.,
Lamb, John A.,
Ledford, James W.,
Larkin, Fay,
Ledyard, Robert L.,
Micou, Paul I.,
Miller, William H.,
Menefee, Thomas B.,
McClung, Benjamin F.,
Massengale, William L.,
Murphree, James S.,
McQueen, William P., Jr,
Mulcahy, Frank G.,
McGee, Samuel J.,
McDowell, Ray,
Miller, Jesse G.,
McNeill, Benjamin S.,
McKinzie, Alfred J.,
Magna, Angelo,
Mathews, Jessie,
Norris, Charles M.,
Norris, William S,
Owen, Robert W.,
Overton, Albert S.,
Perdue, Eugene A.,
Powers, Rutledge H.,
Pope, Albert J.,
Penick, Lucius,
Rawlinson, Duglas,
Rogers, Henry C.,
Rogers, Archie G.,
Roots, Charles I.,
Ruppenthal, Nathan S. L.,
Smith, James H.,
Smith, William K.,
Smith, Charles A.,
Snell, Tippie A.,
Sheder, Thomas B.,
Sykes, Joseph W.,
Stough, Sidney S.,
Stowe, Claud L.,
Simmons, Lennie P.   Dead.
Thompson, George W.,
Ticknor, Henry W.,
Taylor, Charles A.,
Whatley, Hugh,
Worrell, Albert S.,
West, Ollie G.,
Wallace, William L.,
Williamson, Richard M.,
Weafer, James H.

The Montgomery Greys, known throughout the country as one of the best militia organizations in service, had the inception of its reputation in the Civil War. After the troublous days of reconstruction, it was reorganized and on various occasions rendered signal service to the state in quelling riots and preserving order. When the war with Spain came, Captain May made strenuous efforts to recruit his company with only the most likely-appearing volunteers. He succeeded to such good purpose that when his command left for Mobile, May 2, 1898, it was as fine a looking body of men as had ever marched through the streets of Montgomery. The company was mustered in May 18.

Many of the members abandoned comfortable positions in and around Montgomery under the firm impression that they would see active service within a month after enlisting. Their disappointment on this score was thus made perhaps a trifle keener than that of some other companies, composed in a measure of less prosperous men. But the Greys never wavered in their fidelity to duty nor were they ever lacking in attestations of affection to their captain. Indeed, one of the episodes of interest at Camp Johnston in early May was furnished by several meetings of the Greys at which it was enthusiastically agreed not to take the oath of service unless the authorities would permit Captain May to lead them. These meetings were prompted by the illness of Captain May at the time and the circulation of rumors that the examining surgeons had rejected him. He was given an ovation by his men when he returned to Camp Johnston from the hospital and on his assurance that he would go to the front with them, the company cheerfully went through the muster proceedings.

Company A's official personnel was altered only a few days before the Greys reported at Mobile. Clifford Lanier, Jr., had been captain but resigned that office to accept a majorship in the then Second Regiment, A. N. G. Thereupon, Second Lieutenant H. B. May was elected captain and Jacob T. Bullen was chosen for the vacant second lieutenancy.

COMPANY L.

Phoenix City Rifles.

JEPTHA P. MARCHANT, Captain.

FRANCIS W. HARE, 1st. Lieut.   WILLIAM K. ARMSTRONG, 2nd. Lieut.

Sergeants:

Will D. Wills, First Sergeant.   George Tillman, Q'master Sergeant.
Martin C. Ballou,   Bozemon C. Bulger,
Heath Blanchart,   Norman A. Webster.
James B. Wood,

Corporals:

Beasley M. Jones,   James T. Ware,
Lewis D. Edwards,   William B. Reed,
James O. Posey,   James U. Thomason.

James Alonzo Preddy and E. Jerallie W. Clancy, Musicians.
Walter S. Erwin, Artificer.   William Clyde Simpson, Wagoner.

Privates:

Allen, Raymond,
Alexander, Charles L.,
Amerson, Jefferson C.,
Booth, Reading H.,
Blackmon, Thomas D.,
Bradfield, George T.,
Brown, Fred L.,
Barber, Charles J.,
Bean, William Hugh,
Carter, Sam,
Cartlidge, James M.,
Cartlidge, Sam D.,
Cobb, William Hood,
Cone, Eddie H.,
Coulter, Edward,
Cumbie, James C.,
Crawford, Walter E.,
Duke, James,
Dyer, George,
Dowdell, James F.,
Edwards, Locksla T.,
Elder, Charles,
Elliott, John W.,
Fleming, John R.,
Godwin, John D.,
Goodwin, Lee,
Greene, Richard C.,
Griggs, William P.,
Hanson, Mitchell,
Harris, Tol,
Harris, James W.,
Harwell, Robert H.,
Harrison, Charles T.,
Howle, James T.,
Hayes, Charles A.,
Hickman, George W.,
Hill, William L.,
Holley, Charles W.,
Howard, William,
Hurst, John C.,
Jenkins, Rufus L.,
Jones, Eli,

Johnson, Charles O.,
Jackson, John P.,
Kittrell, Thomas J.,
Kelly, Alfred I.,
Logan, Robert A.,
Lowery, John T.,
Matthews, Thomas F.,
McAlpine, Solomon Q.,
McBryde, Samuel,
Milford, Marcus L.,
McSwain, William,
Murray, Pat.,
Mason, Robert S., Jr.,
Moore, Robert E.,
O'Hara, Ira,
O'Pry, Hugh,
Phillips, Fred,
Phillips, William R.,
Parton, Thomas,
Patrick, John H.,
Power, Edward S.,
Pace, Thomas W.,
Reese, Tobias,
Roberts, Charles E.,

Rion, Frank,
Roan, Forrest T.,
Sayers, James W.,
Smith, Perry,
Smith, William I.,
Stanton, Eddie G.,
Speake, James D.,
Statum, Charles,
Sweatt, Robert D.,
Seymour, Austin B.,
Thompson, Clarence C.,
Varner, John I.,
Valentine, David O.,
Watley, Robert L.,
Walker, Wiley J.,
Whaley, Samuel C.,
Williams, Earl P.,
Williams, Joseph H.,
Williamson, Monroe,
Woodall, Henry M.,
Worsham, Walter H.,
Weatherly, Frederick,
Zimpelman, William F.

The Phoenix City Rifles (Company L) were previously known as the Tom Jones Rifles. After the reorganization, Captain Marchant assumed command and retained it through the volunteer service. There had been some talk of organizing a separate company of students from the military college at Auburn, Ala., but these volunteers joined their fortunes with the Phoenix City Rifles, which were accepted by the governor on May 3, 1898. The company left for Mobile on the following day, reaching Camp Johnston on May 6, with eighty-five men.

B. M. Jones wore the second lieutenant's epaulettes to Mobile, but rejections by the surgeons depleted the company's strength and when William Kirk Armstrong reached the camp with twenty men to fill the command's requisite quota, he was chosen second lieutenant, Jones becoming a non-commissioned officer.

It was said of Company L in the Second Alabama that no more independent set of soldiers could be found. Captain Marchant, peculiarly self-reliant, communicated his spirit to his men and though the company was at all times efficient, the commanding officer of the regiment had reason to know that the Phoenix City volunteers would be among the first in his command to take the initiative in any aggressive company movement. This was illustrated at Camp Johnston. Edward S. Power was then the company's quartermaster sergeant. He went across the guard lines with a soldier from Northern Alabama and after drubbing his opponent, a larger man, was placed under arrest. Captain Marchant investigated the affair. Becoming convinced that as a non-commissioned officer Power should not be confined in the guard-house, the captain notified the officer of the day that unless his prisoner was at once released Company L would decline further duty in Camp Johnston. The captain had already notified those of his men who were on guard to quit their posts and he was engaged in instructing his company not to respond to the drill call, when Power reported to him that he had been released. Of course that was before the company had been mustered in, but in after days Captain Marchant assumed positions no less positive. Once, the captain was reprimanded by the colonel for failing to have a water-hole filled. The captain had already endeavored to fill the hole but a laxity in the camp's police regulations frustrated his efforts. "If you can't have this done, I'll do it," the colonel is reported to have said. "All right, sir; go ahead and do it; you have more men than I have," the captain answered.

Though Captain Marchant was jealous of his men's welfare he was even more careful in requiring a prompt execution of his own orders. But he was indisposed to resort to the tortuous processes of courts-martial. "When any of you have a grievance against me," he once said to his company, "come to me and we'll settle it like men." Once on the drill field at Jacksonville, Fla., a private threatened to strike a corporal. "Hit me, instead," the captain invited; and when the offender made a surly reply the response was a blow on the jaw from the captain's right hand.

And it was doubtful whether any other captain in the regiment had more of the real affections of his men.

COMPANY F.
Warrior Guards (Tuscaloosa, Ala.)

Mustered in by Capt. W. W. Brandon, since appointed Major.

STERLING FOSTER, Captain.

JULIUS LEVINE, 1st Lieut. CHARLES A. WYMAN, 2d Lieut.

Sergeants:

John B. Battle, First Sergeant.
Noble W. Foster,
Charles A. Coleman,
Justin B. Turner, Q'm'ster Sergt.
Charles A. LaBoyteaux,
Samuel J. Cole.

Corporals:

Robert Cornell,
Thornton Parker,
William H. Garner,
Ernest F. Kirkham,
Graham Parker,
James B. Coulter.

Joseph E. McGee, John F. Parton. Musicians.
Robert B. Sapp, Artificer.   Sidney A. Christian, Wagoner.

Privates:

Allgood, Robert S.,
Anderson, Samuel,
Adams, James T.,
Bailey, Joseph C.,
Barton, Aaron J.,
Ball, Oliver O.,
Bealle, Alfred B.,
Bell, Augustus J.,
Black, Joseph F.   Dead.
Booth, David A.,
Booth, Douglas,
Byrd, Daniel H.,
Cardon, Samuel G.,
Chisholm, Ernest J.,
Childress, Robert M.,
Carpenter, John P.,
Clark, John W,
Colvin, Hiram V.,
Compton, Walter H.,
Cox, Edward E,
Crow, James,
Dawson, Manly M.,
Davis, James L.,
Doss, Aubrey K.,
Dulin, Winston W.,
Dunn, William L.,
Ellis, Augustus B.,
Ezell, Levi A.,
Elliott, Andrew J.,
Fairless, Hugh T.,
Fitts, Fairfax,
Foster, Otis,
Friedman, Samuel W.   Transf'd to Hospital Corps, July 28.
Green, Andrew J.,
Holcombe, Junius W.,
Hall, William C.,
Harp, John,
Hood, James S.,
Hulsey, Stephen K.,
Jones, Ves,
Key, Edwin A.,

Kahn, Joe,
Killough, Willie B.,
Kilpatrick, William F.,
Korner, James W.,
Lamb, Robert E.,
Latham, James E.,
Lawhon, Alex C.,
Leach, Edward F.,
Ledyard, Edward,
Lynd, Ben F.,
Madden, John J.,
Malone, Richard,
Mattison, Luther A.,
May, Eugene L.,
May, Henry C.,
Meridith, Reuben A.,
Murphy, Thomas J.,
Miller, Victor C., Regimental Color Sergeant,
McCord, David J.,
McFarland, Douglas,
McMaster, James M.,
McGraw, Benjamin,
Northington, Eugene G.,
Parks, Edward D.,
Painter, William S.,
Payne, Leonard,
Pattie, Robert F.,
Peterson, Hiram S.,
Powell, Hemrica H.,
Rabun, Luther W.,
Randan, Henry,
Riley, Callie,
Robison, Robert A. Honorable discharge, Aug. 10, 1898.
Ross, James B,
Ryan, James A.,
Satterwhite, Joseph L.,
Shamblin, Jacob,
Sims, Sid L.,
Sims, William W.,
Snow, John A.,
Stapp, John D.,
Sumner, Willard,
Stebbins, Charles M.,
Thômas, William M.,
Tutwiler, Edward M.,
Tallman, Thomas A.,
Williams, James,
Wilson, Archie,
Woodruff, Henry C.,
Yarbrough, Edward.

Romance and history vie with each other in lending interest to the record of the Warrior Guards (Company F). It is certain that no other militia organization in the South has a greater age. Indeed, there is no authoritative means of deciding just when the company was organized. But in a copy of the *Daily Intelligencer* of Tuscaloosa of 1829, the following notice is found:

"The Warrior Guards will meet at the market house to-morrow morning at 8 o'clock with twenty rounds of ammunition. Sept. 10, 1829.

"ERASMUS WALKER,
Captain.

"A. H. SOMERVILLE,
"Orderly Sergeant."

There is about this notice a tinge of the early frontiersman's perils. It shows that the Warrior Guards were active in the defense of the community in the days when militia service was a serious duty. Continuing through the stern years that followed, participating in the defensive plans against the savages who now and then sallied from their woodland fastnesses on predatory excursions, witnessing successively the Seminole and the Mexican wars, the Warrior Guards never relaxed their military activity; and in the *Tuscaloosa Observer* of November 21, 1860, the following reference to the organization was printed:

"This splendid company of infantry has returned from the fair at Demopolis, laden with honors. We learn that they bore away the first prize offered to the competitors. The banner is not yet made, as it was thought it would be agreeable to the successful competitors to have some share in the selection of appropriate devices.

"We hope our worthy governor will find it convenient to forward the arms to which this company is entitled, as an army with nothing but banners will not do much service in the 'irrepressible conflict.'"

Under the gallant captaincy of Robert E. Rodes, whose name has since been inscribed in ineffaceable characters on the tablets of fame, the Warrior Guards went forth to battle for the Confederacy. How bravely and how nobly the valorous band acquitted itself will never be forgotten so long as truthful histories of the Civil War are read. It is interesting to know, too, that the first Alabamian wounded in that strife was a member of the Tuscaloosa company—Private E. W. Tarrant, shot in the leg while on picket duty.

In 1831 the company was reorganized with John B. Durrett as captain. From that time on the Warrior Guards have occupied a position in the foremost ranks of the state militia. Henry B. Foster, afterward a colonel in the national guard and subsequently senior major of the Second Alabama Volunteers, served a term as the company's captain. William R. Foster commanded the Warrior Guards during the term 1893-94, when successive strikes and riots occasioned active service at Birmingham and neighboring points.

William Woodward Brandon followed as the company's commander and it is certain that no more popular or efficient officer has served in that capacity. Under his captaincy, the company won the prize offered for the best drilled militia company in Alabama in the summer of 1895.

It was during the command of Capt. Louis Walter in the early '90's that the Eutaw detachment of the Warrior Guards was formed and this auxiliary body has ever since been of the most material value to the main organization.

The Warrior Guards claim the honor of being the first company in Alabama to leave home for the volunteers' rendezvous at Mobile. The company left Tuscaloosa on the night of April 30, 1898, Capt. W. W. Brandon in command, reporting at Mobile with 100 men the following day. May 18, Captain Brandon was appointed major of the Second Alabama's Third Battalion. Up to that time, the Warrior Guards were the senior company of the regiment. First Lieut. Sterling Foster succeeded to the captaincy, Second Lieutenant Levine becoming first lieutenant and Sergt. Charles A. Wyman becoming second lieutenant.

The people of Tuscaloosa, proud of the company and its achievements, tendered a brilliant and elaborate "peace jubilee" in honor of the volunteers' return home. The function took place October 6, 1898, and was attended by a majority of the company's war membership, the entire regiment being on thirty days' furlough at the time.

COMPANY D.
Montgomery True Blues.

C. F. ANDERSON, Captain.

V. M. ELMORE, JR., 1st Lieut.　　　C. A. ALLEN, JR., 2d Lieut.

Sergeants:

T. J. Powell, First Sergeant.　　W. L. Shepherd, Q'master Sgt.
R. F. Trimble,　　　　　　　　　Al. A. Reynolds,
E. F. Baber, Jr.,　　　　　　　　L. J. Chambless.

Corporals:

F. C. Sagendorf,　　　　B. B. Cobb,
Will P. Lay,　　　　　　I. Abraham,
W. E. Lum,　　　　　　Al. Hayhurst.

R. F. Walker, W. T. Dunne, Musicians.

H. Bomm, Artificer.　　　H. McCarley, Wagoner.

Privates:

Alford, William J.,　　　English, John,
Blakely, W. A.,　　　　Elmer, Mason,
Byrd, A.,　　　　　　　Fairey, E. L.,
Brown, R.,　　　　　　Faber, C. D.,
Brown, L. C.,　　　　　Ferguson, E. D.,
Barnett, J. J.,　　　　　Glunt, O.,
Bridges, J. M.,　　　　Gullett, J. E.,
Baer, L.,　　　　　　　Gallaspy, W. G.,
Carr, J. L.,　　　　　　Goodman, J.,
Carr, E. D.,　　　　　　Hurley, R. P.,
Condon, R. W.,　　　　Henderson, J. D.,
Cooper, Sam,　　　　　Hawkins, W. W.,
Clements, Will,　　　　Hubert, Thomas,
Cook, C. L.,　　　　　Hopkins, J. M. C.
Cook, F. W.,　　　　　Jackson, E. E.,
Crandall, Tom,　　　　Jackson, A. B.,
Cogswell, Robert,　　　Lum, H. M,
Dison, B. F.,　　　　　Laster, R.,
Donaldson, O. K.,　　　Lapsley, J. P.,
Dibble, O. C.,　　　　　Lapsley, E. W.,
Dozier, A. M.,　　　　Loftis, B. D.,
Dorough, L. M,　　　　Murray, J. H.,
Dullaghan, C. D.,　　　Murray, W. T.,
Devore, Frank,　　　　Maydwell, F. H.,

Meadows, J. J.,
Morris, L. A.,
Murtishaw, W. H.,
Melton, W.,
Meehan, M. J.,
Mott, J.,
Mollett, Edward V., Jr.,
McArdle, James A.,
McDuffie. E. C.,
McWhorter, T. H. B.,
McManus, F. S.,
McRae, Alex,
McCarley, H,
Nunn, M. H.,
Pearson, J. A.,
Payne, S. F.,
Powell, J. W.,
Robson, H. C.,
Rhodes, R. R.,
Reade, E,
Ross, Joe,
Renfroe, N.,
Smith, D. A.,
Smith, F. D.,
Sherman, C.,
Sherwood, J. M.,
Steed, C. D.,
Simpson, Joe,
Schwab, F. C.,
Somerset, Grant,
Taylor, J. B.,
Taylor, Lee,
Tuttle, Harvey C.,
Walker, A. J.,
West, J. T.,
West, J. K.,
Wood, J. B.,
Watson, Thomas,
Williamson, N.,
Wilson, H. B.

One of the oldest national guard companies in the country was organized under the name of the Montgomery True Blues in 1836. The command volunteered to participate in the war that was then being waged against the Seminole Indians in Florida. As an organization, the True Blues have since offered their services in three wars—to the United States against Mexico; to the Confederate States against the Unionists; and to the United States against Spain.

Some time before the Spanish-American war, Captain Goetter resigned command of the company which was thus left in the charge of these officers: First Lieutenant Charles F. Anderson, Second Lieutenant Vincent M. Elmore and Junior Second Lieutenant Charles A. Allen, Jr., the last office being at that time provided for by the state law. At a meeting of the company held immediately after the president issued his call for volunteers, seventy-five per cent. of the members agreed to respond in a body. First

MAJ. ROBERT B. DU MONT,
COMMDG. SECOND BATTALION, SECOND REGIMENT ALA. VOLS.

PHOTO BY LIVINGSTON, MONTGOMERY.

Lieutenant Anderson was chosen captain; V. M. Elmore, Jr., first lieutenant; and C. A. Allen, Jr., second lieutenant.

On May 2, 1898, the company reported for duty at the Mobile rendezvous and was declared one of the best equipped commands in camp, as most of the men were armed and uniformed, while sixty per cent. of the other volunteers were without military apparel. The True Blues were mustered into the volunteer service on May 20, 1898.

Second Lieutenant Charles A. Allen was afterward appointed regimental ordnance officer and he served in that capacity until the muster out.

COMPANY E.
Gulf City Guards. (Mobile, Ala.)

JOHN D. HAGAN, Captain.

EMILE A. HINES, 1st Lieut.   CHARLES W. MOORE, 2nd Lieut.

Sergeants:

Comer Sims, First Sergeant.
William R. Davol, Q'master Sgt.
Walter Smythe,
Gustave C. Dornes,
Otto E. Toenes,
Moses Koenigsberg,
S. F. Humphries. Discharged.
William F. Fincher (resigned first sergeancy.)

Corporals:

Thaddeus T. Boon,
William V. Jackson,
William B. Kramer,
Charles H. Lenser,
Henry T. Newbold,
Arthur H. Davis, (transferred to Signal Corps.)
Webster Brannon,

Armistead M. Bonham, Joseph L. Lema, Musicians.

George H. Smith, Artificer.   Maurice T. O'Brien, Wagoner.

Charles A. Dumas, Cook.

Privates:

Batchelor, George B.,
Broad, William A.,
Brown, Owen G.,
Barry, Robert, Jr.,
Bolling, Charles A.,
Brix, Maynard L.,
Balurdo, Joseph P.,
Baggett, Jesse,
Brannon, Robert L.,
Blair, Alexander C. (transferred to Signal Corps).
Cummings, Walter,
Campbell, William J.,
Cullum, George J.,
Cottrill, James E.,
Chastang Edward,
Crowell, John A.,
Connally, William F.,
Chilton, Francis E.,
Camp, William H.,
Daly, William J.,
Dumas, Paul,
Dumas, John W.,
DeVol, Harry O,
Dixon, Charles E.,
Dixon, Augustus,
Dixon, Samuel E.,
DeSilvey, Edward,
Day, Frank P.,
Downing, Lee,
Delmarter, Edward,
Esmonde, Charles E.,
Feeney, James,
Ford, Clinton J.,
Farnsworth, Frank,
Foster, Edward, Jr.,
Fredrickson, Edward A.,
Green, Marion,
Gorman, Michael,
Galvin, Michael,

Head, John,
Huband, John A.,
Harris, Benjamin B.,
Hinson, Wallace S.,
Heineman, Alfred,
Herrin, Columbus M. Dead.
Hood, Walter M.,
Johnson, Charles E.,
Johnson, George S.,
Jackson, Christopher M.,
Joynt, Frank. Dishonorably discharged.
Koch, Albert,
Lequire, John H.,
Miller, Edward N.,
McGinn, Walter C.,
McWhorter, Robert H.,
Mitchell, Edward E.,
Minion, John W.,
Muller, Hugo,
Moore, Archie T,
Murphy James F.,
Nichols, Nathan J.,
Newman, Earl,
Pettus, Jesse A.,
Pear, Frank,
Pierce, Robert J.,
Parsons, Joseph,
Reese, Alfred H.,
Rodgers, Henry S.,
Ryan, William A., Jr.,
Richardson, Harry,
Stewart, Charles M.,
Spann, Joseph H.,
Shugrue, James,
Shugrue, Frank,
Stevens, Curtis E.,
Severson, Charles E.,
Silva, Antony J.,
Tucker, Clarence M.,
Turner, George P.,
Townsend, Joseph A.,
Terrill, Clifford L.,
Wagner, Thomas,
Williams, Lawrence H.,
Wallace, David W.,
Wentworth, Harry W.,
Wilson, William B.,
Wells, Henry T,,
Walker, George.

"The fighting company of the Second Alabama"—such was the reputation given the Gulf City Guards (Company E). Commanded by a captain whose reputation for personal courage had already gained exploitation in the national guard, the "Gulfs" were indeed a formidable set of men, drawn, as they were, from robust representatives of all walks of life. Scholar and clerk, artisan and business man met on a common footing in the company street with the unanimous desire to "whip Spain." That Captain Hagan's command contributed a generous quota to the guardhouse contingent or that discolored optics were worn by its members as badges of honor reflected in no way unfavorably on the company. No other command in the regiment drilled more satisfactorily at important junctures or manifested better esprit de corps.

Once at Miami, a member of Company E was arrested for fighting in the quarters of the First Alabama. When Captain Hagan was notified of the arrest, he asked: "Did he whip his man?" "Yes; sir," was the answer. "Then tell the officer of the guard to release him at once," the captain ordered—"If he had got whipped I would have preferred charges against him."

The Gulf City Guards were organized, November 23, 1860, and in the following January were on duty at Fort Morgan. Afterward, when Alabama seceded from the Union, the Guards tendered their services to the Confederacy and, on being immediately accepted, were assigned to the Third Alabama which afterward distinguished itself as one of the crack regiments in the Confederate service.

Immediately after the Civil War, the company was reorganized and participated regularly in all the civic and military exercises of a general character that transpired in Mobile. The following gentlemen have at various times served as captain of the company: O. J. Semmes, G. C. Tucker, C. L. Huger, G. H. Smith, LeVert Clark and E. M. Underhill. Captain John D. Hagan's original commission dates May 1, 1894.

The Gulf City Guards were the first Mobile company to report for duty at Camp Clark, pitching their tents there on the evening of May 5. The company was mustered in, May 21.

COMPANY M.

Mobile Cadets (Regimental Color Company.)

WILLIAM L. PITTS, JR., Captain.

JOHN H. PARTRIDGE, 1st Lieut.   HOWARD GAILLARD, 2d Lieut.

Sergeants:

George H. Jones, First Sergeant.   Thos. E. Clarke, Q'master Sergt.
Henry A. Oliver,   Andrew J. Thompson,
Warren S. Horton,   William F. Jones.

Corporals:

Origen Sibley, Jr.,   Guy J. Belt,
Ralph E. Guin,   Edward M. Riley,
William H. Cunningham,   Isaac D. Toomer.

Edmund P. Cocke, Musician.

Walter J. Bozeman, Artificer.   John C. Johnson, Wagoner.

Privates:

Adams, Frank,
Alexander, Nathan T.,
Arnold, Henry G.,
Bell, William A.,
Belser, John D.,
Bray, Charles E.,
Broadnax, Robert R.,
Boggs, Edward M., Jr.,
Calhoun, Atticus,
Crenshaw, John W.,
Cothran, Edward M.,
Dickens, Smith,
Dunning, William E.,
Dupertie, Samuel H.,
Ellis, Griffin,
Eschmann, Walter,
Friddle, Horace,
Fowler, James J.,
Flynn, John,
Gaillard, John T.,
Harrison, Claud D.,
Howd, Fearl D.,
Hudson, Marion S.,
Irvin, Emmett,
Isbell, Claude,
Jensen, Otto,
Jones, William R.,
Jackson, John W.,
Jones, Patrick A.,
Kennedy, Charles F.,
Knight, Arthur A.,
Meek, Walter,
Mackin, John H.,
McCreary, John A.,
Nilsen, Nils G.,
Newberry, John,
Nelson, James A.,
Nelson, Henry M.,
Newsome, James,
Oakley, William G.,
Oliver, William E.,
Olsen, Anton N.,
Padgett, Robert L.,
Penny, James E.,
Pollard, George W.,
Pugh, Charles M.,

Sharp, George M.,
Singleton, Tandy W.,
Storm, Jacob,
Sullivan, John T.,
Sullivan, William J.,
Smith, Stanley,
Troupe, Jerry J.,
Tuttle, Frank A.,
Tucker, John H.,
Wilson, George E.,

Williams, Henry G.,
Williams, Robert L.,
Woolf, Eugene,
Winslett, Benjamin W.,
Winborne, Wallace.

DISCHARGED.

Charles J. Beasley.

The war with Mexico prompted the organization of the Mobile Cadets (Company M) in 1845. But the command was not permitted to fight the Montezumans. It continued, however, as a militia company until 1861 when, under Capt. Robert M. Sands, it was accepted by the Confederacy and assigned to the Army of Northern Virginia, rendering gallant service in what was then the Third Alabama Regiment. Afterward, when peace was restored, the company was reorganized and on a number of occasions rendered services to the state.

In 1894, the Cadets aided in quelling the labor disturbances at Birmingham. Capt. B. C. Rowan was then in command. Again, in July, 1897, the company was ordered to sleep on its arms in readiness to disperse the mob which, it was feared, might attempt to lynch Isaiah Davis, murderer of Thomas Jones.

April 27, 1898, Captain Rowan, who had commanded the company for three years, called the Cadets together and announced the receipt of a telegram from Governor Johnston, asking how many members of the command could report for duty in the volunteer army at once. A score responded. On May 11, the company marched into camp at Mobile with fifty-six men. Captain Rowan enjoyed the reputation of being one of the best militia officers in Alabama's service and his followers were extremely disappointed when Dr. Purviance announced that he was physically ineligible.

Meanwhile, First Lieut. Thomas M. Stevens, actuated by strong personal reasons, felt constrained to resign.

Then Lieut. W. L. Pitts, Jr., who had been in command of the Nelson Battery (artillery) at Selma, took forty men to Mobile, May 31, and, turning them over to the Cadets, succeeded Rowan as captain, Second Lieutenant John H. Partridge being promoted to first lieutenant, vice Stevens.

One of Company M's sergeants, Thos. Partridge, was given a commission in the colored troops and after his release from the Cadets, promotions followed. Sergeant Howard Gaillard, who reached camp as fourth corporal, was named for the company's second lieutenancy. But First Sergeant Colden A. Brown also sought this commission. His successful opponent was nominated by the commissioned officers and Sergeant Brown, displeased because the contest had not been submitted to the arbitrament of the enlisted men's votes, doffed his uniform and returned to civilian life. This was, of course, before the muster in.

COMPANY B.

Lomax Rifles. (Mobile, Ala.)

DeWitt Camp, Captain.

John P. Moffat, 1st. Lieut.   Thos. F. McKay, 2nd. Lieut.

Sergeants:

George S. McKinney, 1st. Sergt.   Thos. W. Carey, Jr., Q'master Sergt.
Jas. R. Eagon,   William A. McCreary,
Duke Guice,   Walter R. Snead.

Corporals:

John D. Burnett,   Alvin Van Iderstine,
Lonzo A. Gaskey,   Evander B. Evans,
Elijah R. McCreary,   Elmer N. Smith.

Thomas M. Flowers and Ray Sunderland, Musicians.
Charles M. Hogaboom, Artificer.   Miles A. Moody, Wagoner.

Privates:

Allen, Ben. J.,   Ferguson, Fitzhugh H.,
Armstrong, Aristo T., Jr.,   Fowler, Henry R.,
Attaway, Mose,   Gale, Edward B.,
Amos, Charles A.,   Gaynor, James T.,
Benthey, Edwin O.,   Genner, George F.,
Broadus, John,   Gideon, Edgar V.,
Browning. John,   Goldsmith, Walter B.,
Bronzo, Richard L.   Deserted.   Graff, Henderson,
Ball, John E.,   Hendon, Edward T., Jr.,
Benedict, Henry L.,   Henry, Ben. G.,
Buck, John B.,   Hawkins, Charles C.,
Callaway, David R.,   Harwell, Frank,
Cawthon, Byron O.   Deserted.   Hogue, Fred. L.,
Callins, Samuel E.,   Holley, David M.,
Coker, Walter J.,   Hertz, Edward D.,
Carr, Walter T.,   Houck, Wm. J.,
Costello, Allan B.   Deserted.   Hyslop, Thomas,
Crowley, John B.,   Hannon, John S.,
Davenport, Geo. F.,   Hempel, Paul,
Daly, Hugh,   Hansen, Albert,
Evans, William,   Harrison, Arthur J.   Deserted.
Feagin, Charles T.,   Ikner, Theodore N.   Deserted.
Favors, Monroe,   James, Elvin E.   Dead.

Johnson, Wiley T.,
Kennedy. James L.,
Klausen, John P.,
McCreary, Frank R.,
Mahon, John J.,
McGehee, William W.,
Mitchell, William H.,
Minott, Henry W.,
McCracken, Charles L.,
McCormick, James E.,
Monohan, James H.,
Murphy, Patrick,
Murphy, William,
Melia, John J.,
Marik, Charles J.,
McGowan, John,
McLean, Christopher,
Nielson, Samuel,
Nay, Harry,
Phelan, Thomas M.,
Preachers, Philmore,

Robinson, T. Walter,
Rogers, Samuel L.,
Summersell, Charles J.,
Sammereier, Anthony. Dead.
Shobe, Clyde O.,
Shaw, Edward J.,
Skinner, Edward R.,
Smith, Joe,
Smith, Lewis C.,
Smith, Irby T.,
Stone, William P.,
Snead, Albert H.,
Sandiford, John,
Thames, Stephen,
Tucker, Frank D.,
Van Vleck, Victor J.,
Vansickle, Amos W.,
Wells, Alonzo E. Dead.
Willis, Charles E.,
Warren, Augustus W.,
Werthner, Henry A.

DISCHARGED.

Jesse R. Latham.
Walter N. King,
Raymond R. Denton,

Thos. P. Aldridge,
William J. Barnes.

It was in June, 1883, that the Lomax Rifles launched on their national guard career. Two years later the company captured the first prize at an inter-state competitive drill in Washington, D. C. From that time on the Lomax Rifles continued to maintain its militia prestige in such a successful manner that it was known to national guardsmen throughout the country for the excellence of its drills. Frank P. Davis was the first captain, resigning his company command to become colonel of the regiment. In 1885, however, he relinquished the colonelcy to take the company to the competitive drill at the national capital. After that he again resigned. Captain DeWitt Camp, who mustered the company into the volunteer service, June 14, 1898, had commanded the Rifles for seven years.

Once, on that eventful July evening in 1897—since referred to by Mobilians as the "night of horrors"—the Lomax Rifles were ordered under arms to preserve peace. A lynching bee was expected but the company was not required to fire a shot.

When the Hispano-American embroglio was nearing its crisis, the Lomax Rifles became greatly exercised, but under counsel of Captain Camp, nothing was done until instructions arrived from Governor Johnston. Then, May 8, 1898, a meeting was held in the armory hall and a decision reached to volunteer as a company. The command marched to the regimental rendezvous, May 11, 1898. Fifty per cent. of the old members of the company who offered their services were rejected by the examining surgeons. Recruits were obtained from the Conecuh Guards, of Evergreen, whence also came Lieutenant J. C. Snead. He failed to pass the surgical examination, however, and Thomas F. McKay was chosen in his place. The latter had previously served as the company's second lieutenant but relinquished that office and offered himself as a sergeant in order to make room for Snead, who was to have received his commission in recompense for the Evergreen recruits.

From August 26 to September 6, 1898, the Lomax Rifles served on the provost guard at Pablo Beach, Fla., being detached from the regiment for that purpose. The company distinguished itself during this service by its rigid attention to duty. And Private John B. Buck earned a hero's reputation during the stay at Pablo Beach by making courageous and hazardous efforts to rescue Private Reddy, of Company L, Second New Jersey, from a grave in the surf. Reddy drowned but Buck received for his heroic efforts a special commendation by Maj. R. B. Harrison, Provost Marshal of the Seventh Army Corps.

COMPANY C.
Mobile Rifle Company.

EDWARD M. ROBINSON, Captain.

JOHN S. CALLAGHAN, 1st Lieut. DANIEL McNEILL, 2d Lieut.

Sergeants:

Walter E. Urquhart, First Sergt.
Albert S. Williams,
Sherwood Bonner (Promoted Battalion Adjutant),
William J. Primm.

James E. Hood, Q'master Sergt.
Robert E. Austill (Reduced),
William M. McCreary,
Louis R. Benz,

Corporals:

Charles H. C. Hogaboom,
William H. Reynolds,
Conway Penny,

Frank O'Rourk,
William H. Hambrook,
William Briot.

Frederick C. Klem, Musician.

Samuel P. Gilbert, Artificer. William L. Pate, Wagoner.

Privates:

Atchison, John C.,
Ayers, Albert M.,
Barnett, William J.,
Burke, William,
Britton, Bruce C.,
Berry, Carter,
Beeler, William W.,
Buntyn, Harry T.,
Baxter, William G.,
Barbarin, George J.,
Boley, William,
Carter, John,
Cox, Harmon W.,
Case, John H.,
Cunningham, Walter S.,
Donovan, Michael,
Deckhard, Thomas B.,
Espalla, Robert F.,
Ebert, Fritz,
Faulk, Thomas T,
Flournoy, George J.,
Francis, James G.,
Gilberg, Eric E.,

Grove, John F.,
Grassel, Ernest E.,
Godwin, Walter W.,
Gillespie, Stowell W.,
Goos, Fred M.,
Hubbard, Joseph F.,
Harper, William M.,
Hall, Andrew L.,
Hogaboom, George E.,
Hamilton, Willis H.,
Hanna, Frank,
Hellen, Fulford,
Holder, Karl,
Hon, Samuel L.,
Hughs, George B.,
Knauff, William S.,
Keefe, John,
Keefe, Emanuel,
Knoke, William H.,
Love, Henry E.,
Levinson, Henry,
Lamare, Vincent,
Miles, Hudson,

Moore, Peter,
McNab, Henry,
McHugh, Charles A.,
McInnis, Randall L.,
McInnis, Murdock C.,
McInnis, L. B.,
McVey, Walter.   Discharged.
Nocton, James,
Norris, William J.,
Oliver, Samuel W.,
Otis, George W.,
Pelliser, John,
Perryman, Erastus S., Jr.,
Padgett, William A.,
Parshall, George E.,
Rencher, Eugene,
Schooley, Ed F.,
Stanford, Ed S.,
Simmons, Anthony W.,
Steele, Thomas C.   Discharged.
Stowers, Lewis H.,
Sanders, Jodie T.,
Spaulding, Harvey L.,
Schuler, Charles,
Taylor, Jerome E.,
Tate, Charles C.,
Turner, William H,
Urmey, J. H.,
West, Wilie F.,
Williams, Edward C.,
Walker, Charles C.,
Wright, George H.,
Williams, William C. Transferred to Hospital Corps.
Williamson, Sydney P.,
Younger, George.

A right venerable record entitles the Mobile Rifle Company to attentive consideration at the hands of history readers. Organized in 1836 by Captain James Crawford for service against the then hostile Seminole Indians, the company has since shared the fortunes of Alabama with unremitting loyalty. The Spanish-American was the fourth war the company saw as an organization, having passed through, with varying losses, the Seminole War, the Mexican War and the Civil War.

Of course, the command has experienced several reorganizations, but meanwhile its captaincy has been held at various times by men whose names are indelibly written in the history of the state. When the war came with Spain, Captain Edward M. Robinson was Recorder of Mobile. But he decided that he could best serve the country in the field and, resigning his civic position, assumed active command of the company. Like the other Mobile militia organizations, the Mobile Rifle Company was not ready to report at Camp Clark until Colonel Higdon had received a majority of the troops from Northern Alabama. But nevertheless the Rifle Company presented a handsome spectacle as it marched through the streets of Mobile to Colonel Higdon's headquarters on May 6, 1898, and reported for duty.

Both of the company's lieutenants were constrained by powerful personal reasons to resign. First Lieut. John L. Moulton quit his office only with the greatest reluctance. His position was to have been filled by Lieut. W. A. Crossland of Montgomery who agreed to furnish the company with forty recruits. But the arrangement was never consummated. Meanwhile, Lieutenant Moulton served until his place could be filled. Sergeants A. S. Williams, John S. Callaghan and Dan McNeill were candidates to succeed Second Lieutenant Hiram Griffin, but McNeill retired in favor of Callaghan who was elected. Then, when the arrangement with Lieutenant Crossland failed of consummation and Lieutenant Moulton resigned, Lieutenant Callaghan was elevated another notch and Sergeant Dan McNeill became Second Lieutenant.

Captain Robinson and the Mobile Rifle Company figured conspicuously in the history-making of the Second Alabama, but both the commander and the command acquitted themselves with a dignity and creditability at least gratifying. Captain Robinson, as a lawyer, knew the value of an analytical study of army regulations and in this way he gained a relative advantage over not a few other company commanders. The Mobile Rifle Company's affairs were administered in accordance with both the spirit and the letter of the law and the members, readily adjusting themselves to the idea of impartial justice, learned to appreciate discipline.

COMPANY H.
Troy Rifles.

GRAPH J HUBBARD, Captain.

WARREN E. ANDREWS, 1st Lieut.   MARION GALLOWAY, 2d Lieut.

Sergeants:

Josiah Wilson, First Sergeant.   Charles D. Murphee, Q'master Sgt.
Benjamin W. Parker,   Jacob R. McNeil,
Ralph E. Andrews,   Adolphus C. Brannen.

Coporals:

Hugh J. Segars,   George W. Newman,
Benjamin C. Condon.

Samuel H. Parks, Albert N. Crawford, Musicians.
Ernest L. Danzey, Artificer

Privates:

Adams, Daniel M.,   Enzor, Oscar M.,
Armstrong, Hunter H.,   Fortner, William F.,
Arwood, Eudolpher W.,   Frost, Murphy S.,
Baker, Albert M.,   Gibson, Oscar E.,
Boatright, Robert T.,   Gomez, Augustine,
Bronson, Robert P.,   Goodman, Gillis A.,
Blan, Gideon P.,   Gunter, Joseph,
Bower, Orman,   Griffin, Dinkins S.,
Cargile, John F.,   Henderson, Augustus,
Carlisle, Walter E.,   Henderson, John,
Carter, Elias J.,   Hill, Joseph C.,
Chapman, Edmund A.,   Hollis, John O.,
Connerly, Joanna C.,   Harris, Robert C.,
Craddock, William B.,   Horton, William J.,
Collier, Howard,   Jackson, William G.,
Cox, Jesse C.,   Jacobs, Robert M.,
Courtoy, Frederick L.,   Jeter, Frazer L.,
Cameron, ———.,   Jones, Frank R.,
Daniel, Charles O.,   Kelly, James F.,
DeWitt, Robert L.,   Kendrick, James T.,
Darby, Ben,   Kirbo, Homer L.,
Davis, Brunie,   Lawson, Frederick,
Davis, Lee,   Lee, Charles S., Jr.,
Devant, David D.,   Lewis, Henry H.,

Lewis, Robert S.,
Liger, Walter H.,
Malone, Walter J.,
Moody, Bishop M.,
Moody, Harry L.,
Morrison, John,
McLaney, Clayton,
Norton, Sam.,
Newman, William,
Parker, James B.,
Pittman, James L.,
Powell, Samuel T.,
Parks, Adam,
Pinckard, William L.,
Price, R. F.,
Price, J R.,
Reardon, Alger P.,
Rosenberg, Philip R.,
Reppard, Robert E.,
Rhodes, Charles A.,
Slaughter, James A.,
Stephens, Alton P.,
Stewart, George F.,
Stewart, Robert L.,
Strickland, John H.,
Solomon, John L.,
Spivey, William D.,

Townsend, Samuel T.,
Travis, William P.,
Turner, Ulysses,
Taylor, Abraham H.,
Watson, James,
Whitaker, James N.,
Whittemore, Waldo A.,
Wilson, Charles,
Wilson, John W.,
Wright, Dowling,
Warren, Robert B.,
Thrower, William W.,
Carlisle, Malory J.,
Baker, Joseph F.,

DISCHARGED.

Hough, William T.,
Hollingsworth, Ellison P.,
Espy, James,
Stevenson, Thomas.

DESERTED.

Baker, Joseph F.,
Johnson, John W.

It was in 1893 that the Troy Rifles (Company H) were organized. E. M. Shackelford served as the command's first captain and was succeeded by Graph J. Hubbard. The company served at Birmingham in 1894 during the labor riots there.

Some difficulty was experienced in recruiting the volunteers' ranks up to the required company quota and it was not until May 27 that the muster in was accomplished at Mobile, though Captain Hubbard's followers were among the most enthusiastic at the rendezvous, the company having reported at Camp Clark for duty May 4. First Lieutenant C. H. Cowart who went to Mobile with the company was told by the surgical examiners that he was afflicted with an ailment which would be aggravated by army service. He withdrew, therefore, and Warren E. Andrews, who had previous officiated as first lieutenant, was selected in his **place.**

COMPANY I.

Jackson County Volunteers.

CHARLES QUINTARD BEECH, Captain.

GIDEON PRICE BOULDIN, 1st Lieut.   JAS. ROBT. CAMPBELL, 2d Lieut.

Sergeants:

Jas. McCord Skelton, First Sergt.   Felix Robertson, Q'm'ster Sergt.
William Edgar Harris,   Robert Kinkle Harris,
William Rutledge Larkin, Jr.,   John Edward Cotten.

Corporals:

William D. Kelton,   Thomas I. Humphrey, Jr.,
Rufus S. Porter,   Fred Arn,
Charles Rice Caffey.

John Deere, Strauss Edmonds, Musicians.

William Gentle, Artificer.   Jesse A. Proctor, Wagoner.

Privates:

Ashley, Joseph,
Askin, William B.,
Blessing, William F.,
Bouldin, Virgil,
Bynum, Charles W.,
Bauer, George,
Burkhardt, Robert W.,
Coe, Charles W.,
Cotten, Jerry B.,
Cruse, Richard H.,
Cason, John B.,
Coffey, James D.,
Cox, Harry,
Christiansen, George E.,
Coley, Edward J.,
Cummings, Joseph,
Davis, Oscar H.,
Erwin, Joseph C.,
Fehler, John,
Green, Walter D.,
Green, Thomas L.,
Gormley, Lawrence,
Gudenrath, Harry L.,
Gullatte, John A.,
Gattis, Emmet,
Goeber, Isaac,
Gladden, James W.,
Gaines, John,
Goodman, William E.,
Gold, Solomon W. Dead.
Hall, Walter,
Hicks, James M. P.,
Hankins, James M.,
Hancock, James M.,
Hamilton, William A.,
Humphrey, Clare,
Hendren, Starling P.,
Hoffman, Ralph L.,
Hauk, Emil,
Hauk, Alfred,
Hays, Luther,
Herrin, Edward.
Johnson, Herschel V.,
King, William W.,
Lackey, Rice,
Lusk, George W.,

CAPT. E. H. GRAVES,
Co. G, Second Regiment Ala. Vols.

Lewis, John,
Lequire, James C.,
Matthews, Andrew,
Matthews, Lee,
Morris, James B.,
Morris, David A.,
Meade, Lemuel G.,
Moreland, Thomas M.,
McCormack, Benjamin T.,
McCutchen, Harvey B. Dead.
McGann, Alfred W.,
Nash, Jackson,
Owens, Albert,
Oden, Harry,
Parks, Anson B.,
Pickens, John Z.,
Precise, Robert T.,
Precise, James A.,
Potter, David W.,
Ross, James A,
Robinson, John R.,
Selby, Barton B.,
Selby, Walter C.,
Sloan, Tyson M.,
Sisk, Erskine M.,
Sherman, Doc,
Shannon, John A.,
Sutterer, Herman,
Threwer, James M.,
Vicars, John H.,
Warren, Thomas L.,
Warren, Allie G.,
Walker, James R.,
Wilson, John C.,
Wallace, Asa F.

Attired in jeans and homespun, with the untrained gaits of the countryman, the Jackson County volunteers (Company I) appeared at the Mobile rendezvous as one of the most realistically volunteer commands that reported there. On April 28, 1898, circulars signed by G. P. Bouldin, L. E. Brown and Fred Arn, were sent through the mails to Jackson County's youth and chivalry, calling on them to assemble at Scottsboro and "go to the front." On April 30, a meeting was held at the appointed place and fifty-four volunteers were enrolled. An adjournment was then taken and meanwhile more patriots were called upon. At last, on May 2, another meeting was held and thirty additional volunteers subscribed. An election of officers was held and the company left for Mobile, May 3, with instructions to report to Colonel Higdon. The company remained in Camp Clark for more than a week and was then ordered to move to Camp Johnston, where it mustered in under Colonel Cox, May 27.

L. E. Brown, one of the promoters of the company's organization, reported at Mobile as a sergeant, but was rejected because he did not conform with the required proportions of height and weight. Afterward, however, he succeeded in securing the adjutancy of the Third Battalion in Colonel Higdon's regiment.

The Jackson County volunteers' service was tinctured with an unusual degree of disagreeableness. As a purely volunteer company it at first lacked that harmony which comes from continued organization. Earnest work on the part of the officers, however, overcame this difficulty. Still, in the Mobile *Register* of May 17, is found this paragraph: "A special to the Birmingham *Age-Herald* from Scottsboro says: 'Considerable consternation, in fact, indignation, in some quarters has arisen here over the reports that efforts are being made by parties interested to hold a re-election and defeat Capt. C. Q. Beech, of the Jackson Volunteers, now in Mobile. The scheme is generally understood here, and the consensus of opinion is if the plan is carried out, the company will likely go to pieces.' As stated in *The Register* of Sunday, the election for captain of the Jackson County company was held at regimental headquarters late Saturday evening. The election was supervised by Lieutenant-Colonel W. A. Thurston and there did not appear to be any excitement among the men. The opponent of Captain Beech was Lieutenant Bouldin. There were eighty-four votes cast, Captain Beech receiving sixty-eight and Lieutenant Bouldin sixteen. Lieutenant Colonel Thurston then declared Captain Beech the duly elected commander of the company."

But this difficulty was smoothed over. Company I afterward furnished the only instance in the regiment in which an enlisted man struck an officer. The culprit, Joseph C. Erwin had previously served as a corporal. Lieutenant Bouldin caused his reduction and Erwin attributed the incident to personal feeling. Afterward Lieutenant Bouldin took occasion to reprimand him for his non-attendance at drill. Erwin spoke of the immunity from personal violence that the lieutenant's epaulettes conferred. Harsh words passed and the lieutenant told Erwin he "need not bother about the straps." Blows were struck, but before serious damage could be done, both men were seized by other members of the company. Captain Beech ordered Erwin under arrest, but Lieutenant Bouldin declined to prosecute him. This incident occurred shortly before the regiment's removal from Jacksonville, and when Montgomery was reached, Erwin was permitted, like the remainder of the regiment, to enjoy the thirty days' furlough granted, it being understood that the case would be dropped.

Company I shows a larger death roll than any other company in the regiment. Despite its infelicities, however, the company was, as a body, conscientious and energetic in its service.

COMPANY G.
Eufaula Rifles.

G. P. Barr, Captain (Resigned).
E. H. Graves, Captain.

Edgar S. Mitchell, 1st Lieut.   Allen M. Brown, 2d Lieut.

Sergeants.

W. T. Sheehan, First Sergeant,   A. C. Flewellen, Q'master Sergt.,
L. de Lion Harvey,   Leonard E. Adams,
W. M. Petrey,   Bryant Garrett.

Corporals.

Carl Schlich,   Lee Cohen,
H. G Weedon,   Claud Douglass,
Jno. Van Houten,   J. M. Jones,

L. L. Burkhead and E. H. Duke, Musicians.
R. E. Spann, Wagoner.
J. L. Johnston, Artificer.

Privates.

Alston, R. A. Dead.   Gray, F. M.,
Banks, Jim,   Gray, Gus,
Barnes, L. R.,   Grice, S. P.,
Brazwell, L H.,   Goolsby, J. W.,
Brazwell, W. J.,   Harris, J.,
Brown, O.,   Harrison, J. M.,
Brown, J. P.,   Hardman, Jack.,
Brown, A. F.,   Hooten, J. R,
Brown, J. B.,   Hansen, Christian,
Baldwin, J. T.,   Hawkins, O.,
Crawford, J. M.,   Jenkins, T. J.,
Crawford, J. T.,   Katenhead, Geo.,
Canterberry, B. F.,   Kennedy, G. W.,
Caldwell, C. G.,   Kennedy, Edward,
Cumbie, A. E.,   Kaiglers, O. G.,
Cameron, D. W.,   Kirkland, R. C.,
Crutchfield, W. G.,   King, C. C.,
Dickenson, H. P.,   King, D. D,
Dickey, C.,   Kirkland, W. T.,
Daniel, H.,   Lane, N. M.,

McDonald, J. D.,
McKay, W.,
McTyre, T. F.,
Mashburn, T. M.,
Mendall, F. M.,
Miller, F. C.,
Nowland, A. B. Deserted.
Odem, J. A.
Pippen, Geo.,
Penfield, J. W.,
Pruett, R. D.,
Perkins, C. T.,
Pierce, O.,
Parker, J. P.,
Reaborn, C. E.,
Riley, W. L.,
Rollins, W. E. Dead.
Richardson, W. J.,
Roberts, B.,
Seals, M. B.,
Seals, Pope,

Seeets, W. T.,
Sheets, M. C.,
Searcey, J. E.,
Sayers, J. P.,
Stephens, R. K.,
Smith, W. C.,
Taylor, C. L.
Thornton, J. L.,
Thomas, E. J.,
Thomas, T. C.,
Vaughan, N. W.,
Vinson, P. W.,
Wilson, W. L.,
Wolberg, Rob.,
Whitley, F.,
Winslett, J. W.,
Williams, J. J.,
Waterman, L. A.,
Yawn, B,
Yawn, G.,

The Eufaula Rifles were mustered into the state service, September 7, 1897, with seventy-five men, G. P. Barr taking the captain's oath. When Governor Johnston issued his call for Alabama volunteers, in April, 1898, the company held a meeting in its armory hall and decided to offer its services as a body. The Eufaula Rifles reached the rendezvous at Mobile, May 16, 1898, and were mustered in May 31.

Business matters made it imperative for Captain Barr to devote his attention to private interests and when it became apparent that his command would not be required for fighting purposes, he tendered his resignation, September 1, 1898. First Sergeant W. T. Sheehan, Quartermaster Sergeant Arthur C. Flewellen and Allen M. Brown contested for the second lieutenancy, First Lieut. E. H. Graves and Second Lieut. E. S. Mitchell being elevated each one notch by Capt. Barr's resignation. Flewellen received a majority of the company's votes but Brown secured the appointment, though his commission did not reach him until the regiment had encamped at Montgomery.

COMPANY K.

"Vaiden's Rough Walkers."

WILLIAM J. VAIDEN, Captain.

EDGAR HAYES, 1st. Lieut.   L. S. MUNFORD, 2nd. Lieut.

Sergeants:

Oscar Hayes, First Sergeant.   Goodman G. Griffin, Q'master Sergt.
J. Lawrence Finlayson,   David S. Fellows,
George K. Keady,   Seay de Graffenried.

Corporals:

Stiles M. Ulmer,   William F. Temple,
Charles W. Jackson,   James H. Prather,
Alfred J. Kennedy,   Job H. Cunningham.

Aiden W. Cooper, Musician.

Norris A. Tucker, Artificer.   Isaac Gurgainus, Wagoner.

Edward P. Harris, Company Clerk.

Privates:

Amerson, John D.,
Aston, James F.,
Barton, Jack,
Bethea, Triston B.,
Blount, Charles E.,
Braswell, Boliver S.,
Burke, James T.,
Carlton, Walter L.,
Carter, William L.,
Carter, William W.,
Clark, Thomas J.,
Clark, John R. H.,
Conner, William,
Cronier, Edward,
Dabney, Robert,
Dennan, Thomas,
Entreken, Garfield,
Ethridge, Joseph E.,
Ethridge, Thomas W.,
Evans, Caleb R., Jr.,
Faulk, Sidney J.,

Fellows, John J., Jr.,
Fitzsimmons, William,
Fleming, William T.,
Gabler, Jacob B.,
Ganzmiller, George J.,
Gaylor, John,
George, Charles J.,
Grimes, James A.,
Grund, Fred.,
Grubbs, Thomas J,
Guthrie, J. Fred.,
Guthrie, Thomas,
Hard, Jean W.,
Hunt, Eldon W.,
Huskey, Leonidas L.,
Jackson, John F.,
Johnson, Henry,
Johnson, Richard H.,
Johnson, W. E.,
Jones, Edward W.,
Jones, Luther L.,

Lee, Robert H.,
Levy, Sollie,
Lindsay, Robert C.,
Lowry, John W.,
Langston, Charles,
Mathews, Vaughn,
Martin, John T.,
McCart, George O.,
McFerrin, Levi,
McDowell, James,
McKinney, Allison D.,
Meeks, John M.,
Moreland, Robert L.,
Morris, Vincent,
Murfee, John M.,
O'Rear, Sim,
Pinion, Fred.,
Pledger, Charles,
Presley, William L.,
Prather, Zeb V.,
Ray, Sanders W.,
Reed, Sidney,
Redmond, Harry,
Ritchie, John E.,
Romine, George M.,
Ryan, William H. H.,
Shooter, Max G.,
Sims, Luther C.,
Smith, Bascom,
Smith, Charles E.,
Smith, Charles F.,
Smith, Thomas I.,
Sparks, William A.,
Spinks, Windsor A.,
Stanley, John N.,
Stewart, Robert R.,
Steinbiihel, Joseph,
Strange, James,
Terrell, Joseph J.,
Thornton, Oscar L.,
Tice, James R.,
Tipton, Robert. Dead.
Upchurch, Oscar T.,
Ward, William W.,
Williams, John A.,
Wilson, James.

"Vaiden's Rough Walkers" won their nick-name while serving on the provost guard at Jacksonville. The company reached Mobile, May, 24, 1898, as a volunteer organization, having been raised by the officers at Uniontown and Jasper and the surrounding country. The captain had previously served in the national guard as a major and his militia reputation aided him materially in raising the company which was mustered in the service, June 7, 1898.

Throughout its career in the volunteer army, Company K furnished much interest for the entire regiment by reason of its peculiar personnel. The rank and file was composed largely of hardy Alabamians who were much less inclined to shirk work than their more indolent comrades from the larger towns. At Miami, the company's quarters, at first the least promising in the regiment, were converted into a miniature boulevard, stone-ballasted and embellished in such a fashion that men tramped through suffocating heat and dust to view them.

One of the company's boasts at the muster out was that it was the only company in the regiment which could boast of an unchanged roster of officers and "non-coms." No one in the company was reduced. The harmony and comradeship which prevailed, as well as the constant industry and energy of the men, were attributed to the peculiar influence exercised over his command by Captain Vaiden, who seemed eminently fitted to lead just such a body of hardy, hearty men.

None of Company K's men was court-martialed. Captain Vaiden was disinclined to prefer charges against his followers. If any of his men showed a sullenness or unwillingness to discharge his duties he was speedily brought to his senses by firm treatment. Or, if he proved intractable and consequently an undesirable soldier, no obstacle was placed in the way of his desertion. Thus the first sergeant once reported to Captain Vaiden: "I expect a desertion to-morrow, sir." "Very well, sir; report to your quarters," was the answer; and when the first sergeant's suspicions were confirmed, the deserter's name was scratched from the company's roll without ado. In this fashion the company came to show a larger list of desertions than any other command in the regiment—at least a half dozen men abandoning their "Rough-Walking" comrades—but the company's efficiency was in nowise impaired by these losses.

REGIMENTAL BAND

OF THE

SECOND ALABAMA.

CHARLES COE, Chief Musician.   L. OTTOE STUBER, Drum Major.

Morgan C. Story,
Miles P. Nelson,
Mott S. Pond,
Tobe R. Folmer,
George E. Wienard,
George Walker,
J Thomas Summersgill,
John P. Stewart,
Arthur Stewart,
John Burns,
E. Cocke,

John S. Edmonds,
Wade H. Orr,
Sam H. Parks,
Clarence W. Black,
W. Lee Mathews,
Richard R. Pace,
Tup Rushing,
J. Edward Searcey,
Emile B. Hauk,
Alfred Hauk,
Frank Forman.

As an organization, the Second Alabama's band was most successful. At Jacksonville it was voted one of the best concert bands in the Seventh Army Corps. Organized June 14, it was beset by many difficulties before it finally surmounted the innumerable discouragements incident to the absence for a time of suitable instruments and sheet music. From a lot of boys who "blowed by ear"—only four men were able to read notes at the begining—the band was developed in three months into a good military organization, rendering standard compositions such as "Robin Hood," grand selection from "The Oolah," "Santiago," all of Sousa's marches and a repertoire of more than 100 pieces.

This remarkable result was due chiefly to the large experience and constant energy of the leader, aided by the interested co-operation of the regimental adjutant as commander of the non-commissioned staff and band.

Only one member of the band ever reached the guard-house and he was only temporarily confined for a trivial offense. But the music-makers encountered not a few tribulations. Sickness at Miami seriously threatened for awhile to suspend the band's work. At one time five of the bandmen were on the sick-list and the remainder were in such poor physical condition that they discharged their duties only with the greatest difficulty. George Walker, a creditable performer on the slide trombone, was sent to the division hospital at Miami and did not recover in time to rejoin the band. His place could not be filled.

At Miami the band was forced to walk more than a mile to a rehearsing rendezvous, and there the members consumed more time fighting mosquitoes than practicing. There were occasions, however, when some zest was added to these inconveniences. One night the piccolo artist aroused the entire camp with unearthly yells. Comrades found him trying to climb a pine tree. He swore a land crab had seized him by the leg and dragged him out of his tent. The crab was captured in partial corroboration of the bandman's story.

When the band was mustered out with the regiment, the leader went with several of the members to accept in the First North Carolina Volunteer Infantry positions similar to those they had just left. Their musical instruments, twenty-one in number, were turned over to Colonel Cox. These instruments had been furnished the regiment through the good offices of Mrs. W. D. Goodman and the Clara Schumann Club of Mobile. Colonel Cox, with several officers in his regiment, shared a trusteeship, the duties of which were to watch and ward the band instruments until they could be returned to the ladies who had procured them for the regimental musicians' use.

SOUTHERN MARTYRS.

CHAPTER I.

ASSEMBLING AT THE STATE RENDEZVOUS.

TO the women of Alabama is due much of the blame for the state's tardiness in raising its quota of volunteers. "This is not a war with which we can sympathize," said a prominent woman of Mobile in May, 1898. "We cannot sanction the shedding of good American blood for the elevation of negroes who are incapable of self-government. We, of the South, have never been able to honestly accept the darkey as a political or economic equal; and we must leave to the North this thing of freeing Spain's West Indian 'niggers.'"

It was the spirit of the Bourbon that prompted these words—the unreconstructed Bourbon whose wounds had not yet entirely healed; and it affected the urban chivalry. It tinctured with indifference the war preparations in Alabama during the May days. It wound the restraining arms of wives, mothers, sweethearts and sisters around the necks of militant patriots. It cast discredit on the sacredness of the war.

This, together, with the fact that the state's national guard was partly an organization but wholly a travesty deferred the day on which Governor Johnston was enabled to notify the authorities at Washington that "Alabama was ready." Still, in the northern part of the state eager officers had been at work from the inception of the international difficulty. Several weeks before, there had been a reorganization of the state militia and Maj. Elijah L. Higdon became colonel of the Third Regiment, A. N. G., composed as follows: Company A, at Woodlawn; B, Florence; C, Gadsden; D, Anniston; E, Anniston; F, Huntsville; G, Birmingham; H, Bessemer; I, Oxford; K, Birmingham; L, East Lake; M, Vernon, Lamar county.

Colonel Higdon communicated with his company commanders and even before the governor was notified of the quota of soldiers required from the state, officers of the Third Regiment, A. N. G., met in Birmingham and agreed to offer themselves and their commands for service. Cols. James W. Cox and Henry B. Foster, of the First and Second Regiments, A. N. G., respectively, being thus forestalled by Colonel Higdon, were forced to unite their commands for the formation of one regiment. At that time their two regiments were made up as follows:

First—Company A, at Mobile; B, Mobile; C, Geneva; D, Fort Deposit; E, Mobile; F, Mobile; G, Eufaula; H, Troy; I, Greenville; K, Evergreen; L, Pollard; M, Monroeville.

Second—Company A, at Montgomery; B, Talladega; C, Selma; D, Montgomery; E, Uniontown; F, Tuscaloosa; G, Union Springs; H, Alexander City; I, Demopolis; K, Selma; L, Phoenix City; M, Marion.

The governor's call for two regiments of white infantry and an additional battalion of colored men went forth on April 28. Already, anticipative measures had been adopted by the various militia officers. Their men were sounded and in those companies in which majorities agreed to volunteer, energetic efforts were made to recruit the membership up to the requisite number—eighty. Colonel Higdon's regiment was ordered to report at once at the state rendezvous which meanwhile had been designated as Mobile. Then, as the other companies were accepted, they also received instructions to assemble at the Gulf City.

Ten of Colonel Higdon's twelve companies finally reached the rendezvous, one of the Anniston commands and the Vernon troop failing to offer the necessary number of men. The Joe Johnston Rifles of Decatur and the Clark Rifles of Pratt City and Talladega ultimately replaced these two companies.

Governor Johnston had arranged to appoint as lieutenant-colonel of each volunteer regiment a regular army officer. First Lieut. J. B. McDonald, of the Tenth Cavalry, U. S. A., stationed for several years at the military college at Auburn, was at once designated as lieutenant-colonel of the First Alabama.

* * * * * * * * * *

It was a beautiful Sunday—the first day of May—that witnessed the departure of the first contingent of Colonel Higdon's regiment from Birmingham for the state rendezvous. The Magic City's thoroughfares were thronged with eager, excited thousands who gathered to bid the volunteers farewell. It was a touching spectacle that bright Sabbath morning—the streets jammed with gaily dressed, tearful women, solemn-faced men and chattering children unconscious of the occasion's seriousness. There were gray-haired dames and grizzled sires to whom the day was tragic in its reminiscences of that other time when loved kinsmen went forth to find unmarked graves on bloody battlefields.

Feeling was tense. The hour itself was pregnant with historic doings. Dewey was at that moment clearing his squadron for the glorious day at Manila. The country was on the qui vive and the whole world was at attention at the hour when those first Alabama volunteers marched from the armories of Birmingham to the town depot. There were dramatic farewells and pathetic partings. At that moment, none knew what was to follow. War's tragedy prevailed.

In that seething theater of pathos and emotion, sentiment and sorrow, were enacted hundreds of incidents in each of which was written a history. No more picturesque illustration could be given of that day's episodes than the leave-taking of Sergeant Luman S. Handley of the Jefferson Volunteers. His father, pastor of the Central Presbyterian Church of Birmingham, sought for his son's sake to repress the grief that filled him. As a Confederate veteran, he endeavored to set his sergeant son a soldierly example. Calmly and without demonstration, he bade farewell after the young man had taken his place in line. "Be a man—a Christian; be a soldier; good-bye, my son," he said calmly. Then he turned away. The company marched past. Before the minister reached the gate of his home, however, the pent-up emotions burst forth and the tried father gave way to tears. He could preach no sermon that morning; and while the sympathetic congregation followed the substitute pastor's prayers for the departing soldiers, their hearts were with the woe-laden father in the parsonage near by.

It was such an earnestness of feeling that crowded the railroad depots from Birmingham to Mobile with great throngs anxious to bid the volunteers Godspeed. It was this same sentiment that collected an immense concourse in Mobile and prompted it to shout itself hoarse cheering the citizen soldiery.

The eight companies of the Third Regiment, A. N. G., which reached Mobile Sunday night, May 1, were accompanied by the Warrior Guards of Tuscaloosa (Company F, Second Regiment, A. N. G.) whose captain, W. W. Brandon, had striven like a Trojan to be the first in camp. And his was the first command of what afterward became the Second Regiment Alabama Volunteers to reach the state rendezvous. The eight companies reporting with him were: the Bessemer Rifles, Jefferson Volunteers, Birmingham Rifles, Huey Guards, Anniston Rifles, Etowah Rifles, Oxford Rifles and the Woodlawn Light Infantry. Twenty-three volunteers from Talladega, afterward becoming members of the Clark Rifles, accompanied this contingent.

The Joe Johnston Rifles, of Decatur, afterward Company E of the First Alabama, reached camp also on the evening of May 1. It had not been a part of any national guard regiment and was purely a volunteer company.

* * * * * * *

On the day previous, April 30, three carloads of tents and camp equipage had arrived in Mobile from Montgomery. Quartermaster General Barry L. Holt of the state national guard, accompanied by Lieut. S. G. Jones, of the Fourth Cavalry, who had been on duty with the militia for four years, worked industriously to prepare the camp for the volunteers' reception. Lieut. Magnus O. Hollis, of the regular army—since elevated to a captaincy—had been detailed by the War Department to muster in the Alabama volunteers and from the beginning he placed himself in constant touch with the state's national guard executives. With Quartermaster General Holt and Lieutenant Jones he inspected the offered camp sites, Alba's pasture at Frascati on the bay, near Monroe park, being selected. Through the energy of these officers, the arriving volunteers found their quarters practically ready for occupation when they reached Mobile.

On the next day, the Montgomery True Blues and the Montgomery Greys reached camp, pitching their tents in the late afternoon. The Montgomery boys were given an ovation by the volunteers who preceded them to the rendezvous; and from that time on each batch of arriving recruits was accorded a rousing welcome.

Colonel Higdon endeavored to at once organize into battalions the companies ordered to report to him. Under his early plans, Lieutenant Colonel McDonald was given command of the first battalion. The second battalion was to be under Maj. Tom O. Smith; and the third was given to

Major McLeod. Of course, this arrangement was afterward altered. But Colonel Higdon and his subalterns were eager to perfect the organization of their own command in order to settle beyond any question the retention of their promised commissions and to that end they hastened the muster work. In those days it was customary to coddle and cajole the recruit. On his willingness to enlist depended the readiness with which the regiments would be mustered in. Hay was procured for the men's bedding and the following routine of calls adopted:

Reveille	6:00 a. m.
Police call	6:10 a. m.
Breakfast call	6:30 a. m.
Sick call	7:00 a. m.
Drill—First call	7:25 a. m.
Drill—Assembly	7:30 a. m.
Recall from drill	8:40 a. m.
Guard mount—First call	8:55 a. m.
Guard mount—Assembly	9:00 a. m.
Officers' call immediately after guard mount.	
Fatigue call	9:45 a. m.
First Sergeants' call	11:45 a. m.
Recall from fatigue	12:00 m.
Dinner call	12:15 p. m.
Fatigue call	1:30 p. m.
Recall from fatigue	4:00 p. m.
Drill call	4:30 p. m.
Recall from drill	5:45 p. m.
Sick call	6:00 p. m.
Retreat	6:30 p. m.
Supper call immediately after retreat.	
Tattoo	9:30 p. m.
Taps	10:00 p. m.

* * * * * * * * * *

The first encampment of Alabama's volunteers was named in honor of the state militia's brigadier general, Louis V. Clark. The latter and Colonel Higdon exchanged a number of amenities on this score, the regimental orders designating the camp's title and the brigadier general's letter of

CAPT. W. J. VAIDEN,
Co. K, Second Regiment Ala. Vols.

thanks for the honor done him being published in the newspapers to the gratification of all concerned. Up to that time, L. C. Brown had acted as Colonel Higdon's adjutant, but, May 3, Lieut. E. D. Johnston, son of Alabama's governor, was regularly appointed to the regimental adjutancy.

May 3 witnessed the arrival at Camp Louis V. Clark of the Huntsville Rifles, the Wheeler Rifles and the Jackson County volunteers. On the following day the Troy Rifles arrived. From that time on, the various commands reporting for service reached the rendezvous as soon as they had recruited to the requisite quota. Some officers, however, unable to raise the number of men required for a company, sought to "take chances" with their followings and promised to complete their companies in time to muster in. In this way Capt. R. C. McFarland, of Florence, reported to Colonel Higdon with a body of men whom he called the Lauderdale County Volunteers. They afterward became members of the Clark Rifles (Company M, First Alabama). May 5, the governor directed the disbandment of the "Lauderdale County Volunteers" and the Lauderdale men effected a consolidation with the recruits from Pratt City and Talladega, Romaine Boyd becoming captain and McFarland being altogether ignored. The company thus formed (M) was the last required to complete Colonel Higdon's command.

The examining board of surgeons entered upon its duties without delay. The board, as appointed by Governor Johnston, was composed of Dr. W. E. Purviance, a captain in the regular army, stationed during the Spanish-American war at Fort McPherson, Ga.; Dr. W..A. Burns, of Sheffield, Ala., and Dr. W. E. Quinn, of Fort Payne, Ala. The first company offered to the board for physical examination was the Jefferson Volunteers. Dr. Purviance, at the head of the examiners, manifested at the outstart his disposition to exact of each volunteer a faultless physique.

Meanwhile, before Camp Louis V. Clark had been fairly established, two disquieting incidents transpired. Sergt. Hugh Collins of the Birmingham Rifles was shot and killed by a negro, Lewis Reese, May 3; and the next day Private M. W. Eckford, of the Montgomery Greys, was declared to be afflicted with small-pox. The tragic fate of Sergeant Collins was accepted by many as an ill-omen while the dread disease with which Private Eckford was pronounced a sufferer tended to discourage recruits from entering the camp.

But both affairs were developed into sources of regimental benefit through the enhanced morale their conclusions contributed. The manner in which the volunteers were restrained from mobbing Sergeant Collins' slayer crystallized the men's early sense of discipline while the consciousness that a comrade had been taken from among them cemented the sentimental ties that bound the recruits together.

Besides, the reported small-pox case was made the means of showing how danger of epidemic illness should be treated. The Montgomery Greys' effects were fumigated, the company sent out of quarters for a day, their bedding burned, the tents moved and the patient himself isolated in an improvised pest house. After all this was done it developed that Eckford's affliction was merely varioloid.

* * * * * * * * *

The Gulf City Guards marched into Camp Louis V. Clark, May 5, and the next day they were followed by the Mobile Rifle Company and the Phoenix City Rifles. May 6 also marked the decision by the governor of the colonelcy of the Second Alabama Volunteers, James Wade Cox being selected for the office. Walter A. Thurston, a lieutenant in the Sixteenth Infantry, U. S. A., was selected for lieutenant colonel; Henry B. Foster, colonel of the Second Regiment, A. N. G., for senior major; and Robert B. Du Mont, lieutenant colonel of the First Regiment, A. N. G., was made major, next in rank. S. S. Pugh was at the same time appointed surgeon major and G. C. Scott, his assistant, with the rank of first lieutenant.

The following day, May 7, Colonel Higdon notified Colonel Cox that he was ready to turn over to him eight companies as the nucleus for the Second Alabama Volunteer Infantry. Colonel Cox at once repaired to Alba's pasture to superintend the laying out of his regimental quarters. Lieutenant Colonel Thurston joined him without delay. On May 8, Colonel Cox assumed command of these eight companies: Warrior Guards, Troy Rifles, Montgomery Greys, Montgomery True Blues, Phoenix City Rifles, Mobile Rifle Company, Gulf City Guards and the Jackson County Volunteers. All these companies had reported for duty to Colonel Higdon, but having belonged—with the exception of the Jackson County Volunteers—to the First and Second Regiments, A. N. G., were reserved, in accordance with Governor Johnston's plans, for the Second Alabama Volunteer Infantry.

Colonel Cox's first order, dated May 8, directed that reveille be sounded at 5 a. m.—he required that the men arise an hour earlier than before. The same order named the camp in honor of the state executive, Joseph F. Johnston. The Second Alabama's quarters adjoined those of the First, a shallow trench dividing the two regiments. The eight companies taken in charge by Colonel Cox were not forced to move their quarters under the new order of affairs, their company streets having been so laid out that no encroachment was made on the First Regiment's reservation.

CHAPTER II.

SOURCES OF INCOMPETENCE.

OF the 1,800 members of the Alabama National Guard, less than 1,200 volunteered; and not more than half of them succeeded in passing the physical examination. It became necessary, therefore, to recruit the regiments from among men who had no conception of the technique of military service. These volunteers were willing patriots, however, and applied themselves to the drill work with an industry and attentiveness that in many instances rendered them superior as soldiers to men who had served years in the militia. But these "raw recruits," though composing sixty-seven per cent. of the regiment, or outnumbering the national guard volunteers two to one, were given no voice, except in a few instances, in the selection of the officers. On the other hand, the militia captains and lieutenants were commissioned by the governor as the "elected officers of their companies." In many cases, these appointees were chosen months before, not because of fitness for military leadership, but because they were popular with the members of their companies, a majority of whom afterward either declined to volunteer or were ineligible for army service. The assertion has been made that the recruits could have chosen between the company commanders already elected and thus enjoyed a broader scope of selection than otherwise. But this is not true. A volunteer, once found, was hastened to camp and held by "right of discovery" in the quarters of the company to which his discoverer belonged. Before the recruit had an opportunity to judge whether he would prefer to follow this officer or that one, he was credited to the company commander responsible for his entrance into camp and that settled the volunteer's fate.

In those instances where elections were held after the rendezvous was reached, matters were conducted in a method no more equitable. Political influence instead of personal merit decided the issue in most of the elections, while in some instances no secret was made of the fact that commissions were sold—bartered for the money necessary to raise a stipulated number of recruits. Companies lacked sufficient men to be mustered in and outsiders' offers were accepted to fetch the necessary number of volunteers to camp on condition that they, themselves, be given offices. The injudiciousness and unfairness of this course were accentuated in several cases by the surgeons' rejection of would-be commission-buyers, indicating clearly that offices had been promised men without any investigation as to their fitness.

All these things tended to detract from the dignity of volunteer officers' positions and to impart to the rank and file a certain contempt for the shoulder strap. Soldiers learned to respect the personality of able officers and to flout the authority of inferior ones. The man and not the epaulettes won respect. In the volunteer army, officers of the same rank were obeyed with varying degrees of promptness. Relative merit won for them relative obedience.

* * * * * * * * * *

This situation was largely due to the flagrant violation of Alabama's military law. Commissions were issued to men who technically and legally were not entitled to them.

Section 2883 of Chapter 76 of the Military Laws of Alabama under the caption, "All officers to be commissioned by the governor; qualifications," prescribes:

All officers shall be commissioned by the commander-in-chief, and no person shall be commissioned in the Alabama National Guard who is not a citizen of this state nor above the age of twenty-one years, *nor until such officer shall have passed a satisfactory examination before a military board which shall be appointed by the brigadier general*, to consist of not less than three members, who shall have the power to compel the attendance of witnesses, administer oaths and take testimony as is possessed by general courts martial, and no person shall be eligible for election or appointment to office in the Alabama National Guard for a period of sixty days after he shall have been reported adversely by the examining board. The report of such examining board must be forwarded through the proper military channels to the commander-in-chief; Provided, that nothing in this section shall apply to the staff of the commander-in-chief.

More than eighty-eight per cent. of the Alabama National Guard officers who were serving in the spring of 1898 held their positions in violation of the state's military laws, or, more correctly, were not legal officers. A large proportion were furnished with "temporary commissions" issued by the adjutant general of the state—commissions that were not commissions at all. Others were serving under commissions made out before the enactment of the foregoing law. But even they had failed to undergo the examination that was also required under the old order of affairs. Less than a score of the officers who were installed in the Alabama Volunteers "on transfer from the national guard" had been entitled to regular bona fide commissions in the militia. The others had failed to undergo the required technical examination. Indeed, it was bruited about as an open secret that an officer who unsuccessfully endeavored to pass this examination in June, 1897, was afterward commissioned in the First Regiment Alabama Volunteers.

Section 2883 of the Military Laws of Alabama was evidently designed to insure official competence in the state militia; and yet its spirit and intent were ignored.

There should have been small wonder then that men of intelligence, gossipping in the volunteer camps of Alabama, opened their eyes in astonishment when told that no provision had been made for mental or technical examinations of their leaders. These recruits knew that a number of the officers looked forward to service in the volunteer army as a source of revenue. Men whose civilian pursuits had yielded them less than an average of $80 per month were eager to enter into a sort of compact with the government assuring them salaries of from $1,400 per annum up. Commissions in the army meant to such men a considerably greater monthly earning than they had ever made before or than they would be likely to make when returned to civil life.

"A man who can't earn $125 a month at home, where there are so many more fields of work, certainly should not be able to make that much in the army," philosophically reasoned some of the patriot soldiers. And in this logic lay the index to the sources of incompetence in the volunteer army.

An army officer's pay is gauged according to a minimum scale of reasonable recompense for the intelligence and ability required for the discharge of his duties. Education, judgment, mental activity and a knowledge of men and affairs are among the chief requisites of an officer. If he has these, then he should surely be able, by applying them in professional or commercial directions, to earn as much in civil life as in the army.

But merit and competence figured as little in the appointment of the volunteer commanders. Under the instructions from Washington, national guardsmen were to be given the preference in acceptances for service. No attention was paid to the fact that Alabama's National Guard was more a farce than a fact. The selection of officers was made the vehicle for profit to men who could present no more important grounds for preference than that they were members of a set which annually cost the taxpayers a sum ostensibly devoted to military purposes but really expended for useless show.

Still, this fallacy was part of the mistake that the commonwealth had indulged for years. It was reflected in the system of "promotion by rank" that obtained in the national guard itself. It was all part and parcel of the absurd error that permitted an intelligent people to confound the importance of soldiery with the subterfuges of politics. It owed its origin to that condition of popular sentiment which opposed military institutions and yet encouraged the maintenance of a dangerous though useless substitute.

Brass buttons and showy uniforms, taken through the set movements of close order drills, had convinced the people that the national guard was a powerful military reserve. It was not in general cognizance that close order evolutions, the spectacular formations on the parade grounds, were more picturesque than serviceable. People believed that, because Alabama companies had distinguished themselves at competitive militia drills, the state was well equipped to furnish a considerable quota of men practiced and finished in the science of war.

The undeception came with the call for volunteers. Not only were the majority of the state's national guard unwilling or unfit to answer their country's call, but the small proportion who did enter the pariot army were little better trained for war than the rawest recruits. True, many went through the manual of arms with the preciseness and accuracy of so many marionettes. But they had been taught practically nothing of the real practice of war—of pointing, aiming and firing their arms. And they knew even less of the duties of a soldier in active service. Extended order— the battle formation—was really novel to them. All were ignorant of the meaning and purposes of outpost duty.

And the line officers—infinitely more time was consumed by them in learning the details and logical sequence of the various extended order formations than the rank and file required to master the mechanical method of execution.

* * * * * * *

Before either Alabama regiment was fairly launched on

its volunteer army career a glaring example of subsequent incompetence was given. No sooner were the officers satisfied of the security of their commissions than a widespread disposition became evident to lounge. Many appeared to consider that they were merely drill-masters, forgetful that such positions were more properly in the sphere of the non-coms. There was but little eagerness to enhance the comfort of the enlisted men and less industry in seeking to protect their health. Orders were ignored. Men lived in the ephemeral conditions of today; naught was done for the morrow. Thus, no safe-guard was thrown around those things that imperil the cohesiveness of an inceptive army. Such a thing as the promotion or enhancement of morale seemed foreign to the line officers. Many appeared to think that the scope of their official duties ended with the perfunctory performance of daily routine.

Official circulars were treated a good deal like so many advertising pamphlets. Thus it was on May 8 in Colonel Cox's first regimental order the following paragraph appeared:

"The commanding officer desires to call attention to the very dangerous trifling with sentinels that has been noticed. A sentinel is the most highly respected officer in the regular army of every nation on earth. His power is supreme and even the commanding officer in any army obeys his injunctions, when the sentinel does not recognize him. We are here preparing for a duty which requires a sentinel to kill any man who does not obey the orders that he is directed to carry out, and hereafter any man found trifling with a sentinel will be severely and summarily dealt with. Special orders will be given the guard for conduct of sentinels on post."

The lines were read and dismissed as though there were no more significance attaching to the phrases than was contained on the surface. Few officers discerned that the sentences enjoined a change of conditions—a change that each wearer of shoulder straps should have aided in bringing about. Instead, guard duty was imposed on offending volunteers as punishment. No plan could have been adopted in such a body more prejudicial to good sentinel service. The spirit of the commanding officer's order was violated. The sentinel was debased, not dignified. The recruits, slow to see the seriousness of camp life, were impressed with the idea that guard duty was punitive. The guardsmen themselves thus became subjects of levity; their posts were looked upon as prisoners' pens. Men were reluctant to serve as sentinels. Being inclined to disrespect guardsmen, they were loath to become subject to such disrespect from others.

Moreover, guard duty became an onerous task rather than an intelligent office. Sentinels were perfunctorily assigned to posts with kaleidoscopic ideas of duty. When the day of muster out arrived there were not 100 men in the Second Alabama who could recite the general orders for a sentinel. Such cursory instruction as was given in the early service was confined largely to the catechism of compliments. More time was devoted to teaching the sentinels how to salute officers than in instructing them how to halt trespassers and possible foemen.

* * * * * * *

The First Alabama was superior to the Second in this relation. Indeed, from the beginning it was apparent that the two regiments differed largely in governing material. In the First Alabama there was manifest an initiative spirit on the part of a majority of the officers together with a disposition to act in concert. But in the Second there was little evidence either of aggressiveness or mutuality. This may be attributed in a measure to the superior opportunities afforded the First Regiment officers in the early camp days to arrive at a common understanding. In after months, these officers accounted much of the regimental efficiency as due to the dominant personality of Lieutenant Colonel McDonald. The latter joined the regiment with a record sufficiently brilliant to command for him the earnest attention of men and officers alike. As a commander of scouts in the West, he rendered distinguished service, being credited with much of the more important work that resulted in the surrender of the notorious Geronimo. Of course, the recruits looked up to him with expectant interest and his task of accomplishing the work set out for him was thus facilitated.

To precisely what agencies the difference between the two regiments can be justly assigned is not certain; but true it is that there was an important and significant difference. Thus it was that in the First Alabama, non-commissioned officers found much less difficulty in discharging the duties of their positions than did the non-coms of the Second. Though there has been much speculation as to the reason for this, it is easily found. In the First Regiment the enlisted men were promptly acquainted with the authorities and respective ranks of their officers, commissioned and non-commissioned. No doubt was left in the minds of any in the regiment as to the obedience and respect due those in authority.

Warrants were issued the non-commissioned officers of the First Alabama Volunteers before the men left Mobile. No warrants were issued the non-commissioned officers of the Second Alabama, save in response to a half dozen requests, up to the time the men reassembled from their thirty days' furlough for muster out. And this omission in Colonel Cox's regiment occurred despite the fact that army regulations prescribe, in mandatory language, that warrants shall be issued non-commissioned officers within three months after their appointments.

In such organizations, where merit or ability alone were seldom the purchases to office, a large, printed sheet with formal verbiage and imposing seals was as much necessary to win obedience for non-commissioned as for commissioned officers. And this was the case particularly because inequitable tenure of authority among the volunteers extended to the stripes as well as the straps. The sprinkling of national guardsmen were eager to divide all the honors and emoluments among themselves despite the fact that they were outnumbered by those volunteers who had never been militiamen. And national guard officers, in sympathy with national guard enlisted men, fostered this plan. Thus a man who had served as a non-commissioned officer in the national guard was frequently promoted "according to rank." Earnest volunteers, who had expected that promotions would be made according to relative merit and ability, became discouraged and disgusted. "We lose opportunities now," some of them said, "because we were not 'tin soldiers' before."

But the inefficiency of volunteer officers did not reflect on their personal capacities. Even among those who seemed least fitted for their positions were men with abundant possibilities. Stout hearts and willing hands characterized perhaps ninety per cent. of the Alabama Regiments' official personnel. But a thoughtless people had failed to provide a proper training for their militiamen; and the sorry spectacle that followed the call to arms was the result of this thoughtlessness. Had the Alabama volunteers who wore straps been properly trained in the militia, they would have accomplished immeasurably better results in the national service.

CHAPTER III.

CAMPS CLARK AND JOHNSTON.

WHILE the work of recruiting the regiments up to the requisite quota was in progress, a number of incidents occurred to engage the more buoyant interests of the encamped volunteers. Though the women of the state had discouraged kinsmen and friends from offering themselves for service, their true mettle asserted itself when the troops commenced to assemble. To the considerateness and charity of the women of Alabama, hundreds of volunteers owe weeks of relief from illness and pain. More comfort was taken to the volunteer camps in womanly hands and on womanly lips than came from both the state of Alabama and the federal government. But the women did not stop with substantial contributions. They lent moral aid, encouragement and inspiration. The men of the First Alabama can remember no army experience more felicitous than the presentation of their regimental flags—handsome, silken banners, hand-painted and embroidered—at Camp Clark on May 7, 1898.

It was an impressive ceremony, celebrated as the parting sunlight painted the tawny bosom of the neighboring bay with a ruddy glow. The banners were given by the women of Birmingham. Miss Louise Chisholm, a beautiful young lady of the "Magic City," presented the flag. She spoke with the dramatic effect that the moment and the scene joined in lending. The earnestness of her words lent a charm to the situation. Briefly, but expressively, she said:

"Colonel Higdon and Soldiers of the First Alabama Regiment: I come from the women of Alabama, your mothers, wives and your sisters, to bear a message and to present a gift which should inspire you to heroic deeds in the camp and on the battlefield, to protect and defend which should be your highest ambition. You, sons of a race destined to rule the world, the gallantry of whose fathers impressed a wondering world,—to you I present your colors, the flag of our country, symbol and sentiment of a united Union, emblem of a constitution made forever sacred by the blood of your fathers in the cause of humanity—we present you this flag.

"The valor of a hundred battlefields will tell you how to guard it. It was never raised but for liberty, it must never trail in dishonor. Glorious sons of Alabama, I envy you your privilege. May the God of Battles ever keep you in His charge, and when you come back the women of Alabama will greet you."

Not one there but in whose memory the scene impressed itself with photographic vividness. Each man and woman in that assemblage felt he or she was part of a historic picture which might in a few weeks receive a crimson setting of patriot blood. The enthusiasm that prevailed was tempered with a deep under-current of solemnity. As Miss Chisholm handed the flag to Colonel Higdon, the Eleventh Infantry, U. S. A. band, loaned for the occasion, struck up the "Star Spangled Banner." The depth of feeling that moved the gathering was reflected in the spontaneity with which the assemblage reverently uncovered as the national anthem swelled forth. Colonel Higdon spoke briefly and then Chaplain Fitzsimmons responded to the Birmingham women. John Kimball, of the Jefferson Volunteers, then acting color sergeant, bore the banner into the ranks of a battalion picked from the regiment to receive it. "Dixie" followed the "Star Spangled Banner."

Then, another beautiful Birmingham girl, Miss Bertha Lewis, presented to the regiment a stand of colors. Stepping forward, Miss Lewis addressed Lieutenant Colonel McDonald. "More than thirty-five years ago," she said, "the devoted women of the South placed in the hands of their husbands and brothers the 'Stars and Bars,' under which the Confederate soldier earned sad, but glorious military fame and honor, in a brilliant but hopeless contest against the 'Stars and Stripes.' The same heroic devotion which animated our fathers in what they believed was a righteous cause against 'Old Glory,' prompts their sons of to day to shoulder their guns and march forth to uphold the honor of that same flag whose starry folds now wave over a united people; and as the prayers of our mothers were offered for those old soldiers, so do our prayers and blessings go with you, the brave soldiers of our state, in this struggle. As a slight expression of our love and devotion for you and the cause for which you battle, the women of Birmingham present you with this flag, the standard of our beloved state. May its bonny folds always wave over a brave and victorious army; and when on the dreary march or amid the boom of cannon and the hiss of bullets you look upon this standard, every stitch of which represents a woman's blessing and whose every thread is sanctified with woman's prayers and tears, remember that the love and belief in you of your mothers, sisters, wives and sweethearts urge you to a brave and honorable discharge of your duty; and their prayers are offered up for your safety and welfare. Take it, and may you sustain the honor, as your fathers have done, and as your mothers would have you do; and when you return, which God grant may be soon, though it may be worn and tattered, all Alabama will point to it as the standard of the noble First, which never trailed in the dust nor lagged behind; and the smiles of Alabama's daughters will greet you as their highest hopes now follow you."

Lieutenant Colonel McDonald answered eloquently, the tone and spirit of the women's words finding earnest response in the thoughts he spoke. He, too, was a Southerner;

and he was proud to be with an Alabama regiment which, he was convinced, would shed their last drop of blood in defense of the colors.

The scenes and circumstances of patriotism that followed these speeches and made the night of May 7, 1898, one of the most remarkable in Camp Louis V. Clark's history were indelibly impressed on the memories of the Birmingham party which traveled 300 miles to attest their devotion to the First Alabama. The party, which reached Mobile over the Louisville & Nashville railroad, was composed of Mrs. Charles G. Brown, Mrs. F. M. Adler, Mrs. A. O. Lane, Mrs. Zack Smith, Mrs. E. L. Higdon, Mrs. T. O. Smith and Mrs. H. B. Catchings, Miss Louise Chisholm, Miss Bertha Lewis, Miss Eloise Ball, Miss M. Lane, Miss Kathleen Hundley, Miss Sadie Hawkins, Miss Ella Hubbert, Miss Tessy Fraleigh, Miss Phelan, Miss Helen Ehrman, Miss Belle Daugaix and Messrs. C. G. Brown, F. M. Adler, H. B. Catchings and Capt. J. B. Merson, of the Birmingham cavalry troop. Misses Belle Daugaix and Helen Ehrman served as maids to Miss Chisholm; and Misses Kathleen Hundley and Eloise Ball performed a like office for Miss Lewis.

A reception at the regimental headquarters and abundant opportunities for the men of the regiment to receive the sweet consolation of womanly sympathy converted the camp for that evening into a haven of hallowed inspiration. Then came the morrow of growing misery.

* * * * * * * * *

Of the life that characterized the Alabama Volunteers' camps in those days, a soldier poet has since essayed these descriptive lines under the title, "Camp Life in a Nutshell":

> Singing ballads, playing cards,
> Eating sidemeat, running guards;
> Marching, drilling, exercising,
> Lying 'round philosophizing;

CAPT. JOHN D. HAGAN,
Co. E, Second Regiment Ala. Vols.

THE NEW YORK
PUBLIC LIBRARY

ASTOR LENOX AND
TILDEN FOUNDATIONS.

Digging ditches, learning tactics,
Standing guard until your back aches;
Doing laundry, picking trash up;
Cleaning camp and dishing hash up;
Cooking pork and taking baths,
Eating hardtack, cleaning paths;
Getting yellow as a tanyard,
Wondering when we'll meet the Spaniard·
Getting letters from our folks,
Snoozing, "boozing," cracking jokes;
Thinking of the folks—if not them,
Then of sweethearts—those who've got them
Reading papers, reading books,
Fasting, grumbling, "cussing" cooks;
Writing letters, cleaning tents up,
In our trousers sewing rents up;
Stewing, growling, fretting, fussing,
Kicking, howling, working, "cussing;"
Drilling like old-time cadets,
Smoking pipes and cigarettes;
Telling stories, making wishes,
Splitting wood and washing dishes;
Turning in at sound of "taps,"
Spouting verse and shooting "craps";
Wanting fight with Spain's "conceitos,"
Getting it with big mosquitoes;
Taking quinine, sick or well,
Castor oil and calomel;
Running out to see the "dummies,"
Calling one another "rummies";
Getting up at five o'clock,
Wanting fight and hearing talk;
Thinking we are not in clover,
Wondering when the war 'll be over.

—Fred W. Raper,
Private, Co. M, First Alabama Volunteers.

But this jingle is optimistic. It does not mention the absence of adequate food and raiment, the scarcity of shelter and the lack of proper medical attention. It says nothing of the distresses and inconveniences imposed on the Alabama Volunteers by the slipshod, hap-hazard methods the government adopted in accepting their services and mustering them in. The men who lived in Camps Clark and Johnston from their establishment to their abandonment will find vast quantities of unintended irony in this extract from a circular letter sent out by Colonel Higdon on May 1, 1898, to company commanders:

"Each enlisted man will be required to have: One small Bible; two woolen blankets (single); two knit undershirts (woolen); two pairs drawers (knit); four pairs socks (light woolen); two towels; one housewife, with needles, thread and buttons (preferably patent bachelor buttons); six extra shoe strings; one pair suspenders; hair brush and comb; clothes brush; tooth brush and tooth powder; razor, brush, strap and small glass; soap and soap box; pencil, paper and stamps."

A majority of the men arrived at Mobile with only the clothes they wore.

* * * * * * * * * *

There had been an excess of jubilance during the early camp days. Those who reached Camps Clark and Johnston before May 10, 1898, seemed to regard their enlistment as a huge outing on which there would be mingled felicity and danger, the latter only enhancing the former. There was no limit to their exuberance. It was "huge sport" for them to parade through the camps in noisy, shouting, yelling, screaming, singing crowds whose only purpose seemed to be to evince their delight in the most boisterous fashion possible. Taps would suspend but not subdue these orgies. From one end of camp to the other bursts of laughter and raillery echoed from tent to tent until approaching dawn brought with it exhaustion. Reveille would find the previous night's revelers hoarse and tired but retreat witnessed their recuperation and a resumption of the clamorous programme. Then followed the gradual accession of painful soberness—the realization that things were not so joyous as had been expected. Continued absence of satisfactory food and adequate clothing and shelter converted jollity into anxiety.

* * * * * * *

The food was worse than that afterward furnished during the most trying period of the two Alabama regiments' history. When Gen. W. M. Graham testified before the War Investigating Committee, October 12, 1898, concerning the conditions at Camp Alger, near Washington, D. C., he might accurately have made the following language refer also to the Alabama volunteers : "While the commissary supplies were plentiful, the men were often without the prescribed rations, because the regimental officers were not sufficiently impressed with the importance of drawing their food. This was especially true in the matter of fresh meat. In one case an officer of a Kansas regiment had refused to draw the fresh beef rations until he could have a saw with which to cut it up." The general also found many of the volunteer officers to be ignorant of the methods of preparing the requisitions.

It is interesting to know that in September, 1898, at Jacksonville, Fla., Capt. F. W. Cole, quartermaster for the First Division of the Seventh Army Corps, in response to questions, said to the writer : "Such distress as has been occasioned in the Alabama regiments by the absence of rations or their tardiness in arriving in camp has been due to the ignorance or incompetence of volunteer officers who have persistently disregarded the set rules for the drawing of supplies."

But the food situation at Camps Clark and Johnston was complicated by a multiplicity of untoward circumstances. First, it was understood that the government would allow only six days' rations for recruits between the time of their arrival in camp and their muster in. This, of course, made the situation embarrassing not only for the recruits but for the regimental officers and the regular army men on detached quartermaster's duty with the two regiments. The most aggravating feature was the total ignorance of the militiamen concerning economization of supplies. Inexperienced quartermasters and incompetent cooks rendered these conditions distressing.

It is true, however, that many of the volunteers strove industriously to improve the arrangements but lack of proper training frustrated their efforts. For awhile, negro cooks were employed but even this experiment was not satisfactory. The recruits having entered camp, fresh from the comforts, conveniences and amplitude of domestic life, expected as good sustenance as they would receive in barracks. And there was no tenable ground for giving them food inferior in quality or quantity. But as early as May 16, a conservative Mobile paper published this paragraph: "There is considerable complaint about the fare among the men of the Second Regiment. One company claims that it had nothing for supper last night but bread and coffee without sugar."

Subsequent developments showed that much of the responsibility for the inferior fare rested on company commanders who not only failed to detail the most competent cooks available, but absolutely neglected to observe the regulations which require frequent inspections of the kitchens and the meals served the enlisted men. Indeed, the writer, from personal observation, is prepared to say most positively that not more than three company commanders in the Second Alabama obeyed the order requiring that they visit and inspect their company kitchens three times each day. Thus, as late as August 11, 1898, complaints reaching the commanding officer impelled him to include this paragraph in a circular: "The old order relating to visits by company commanders to kitchens three times a day is still in force and the commanding officer feels that to call your attention to the fact is sufficient."

But the colonel's hints were seldom effective in the Second Alabama.

*   *   *   *   *   *   *

Dissatisfaction in Camps Clark and Johnston sprang from a dozen different sources. In the latter camp, discipline was delayed through laxity on the part of commanding officers. Anxious to retain full company strength until the muster in was accomplished, they were reluctant to punish men for breaches of order—they feared a stringent enforcement of regulations would disgust recruits and prompt them to desert. In this way earnest volunteers suffered injustice and hardship. Men living in the vicinity of the camps were accustomed to spend most of their time at home or in the society of friends. "Running the guard lines" became the most common indulgence among the volunteers. The lack of dignity with which the officers themselves treated guard duty only added to the inefficiency of the sentinels; and it was an easy task to slip in and out of camp. Thus, when duty rosters were made up, men absent without leave escaped work while those who remained in camp were chosen for tours from which they had already earned relief. Loyalty and attentiveness became the title to hardship; disobedience won excuse from duty. It is no wonder then that many men became chagrined and disgusted at the outstart. Eager recruiting agents and officers had assured them that the government's issue of equipage was already at the rendezvous; that only a few brief formalities separated the recruits from the regular allowance of uniform and clothing. And men who reached camp found that not only was the army clothing weeks distant, but that few blankets and less shelter were provided and that the absence of discipline worked injustice on those who attempted to serve dutifully.

Weak officers were disposed to be lenient, oblivious that in their leniency lay unfairness. Lack of proper instruction, ignorance of men and affairs and inexperience with things military found them unconscious of the fact that, in the army, equality and justice can be had only by a uniform enforcement of discipline.

Volunteers became doubtful as to the wisdom of taking the oath of service. Men commenced to desert before they were mustered in. The following significant order indicates the condition of affairs at that time:

Headquarters First Alabama Volunteers,
Camp Clark, May 14, 1898.

Orders No. 10.]

Company commanders who have men in their ranks who have passed examination and who have refused to be mustered will cause said men to be confined in the guardhouse and report same to the regimental commander. By order of Colonel Higdon.

E. D. Johnston,
First Lieutenant and Adjutant.

CHAPTER IV.

RECRUITING THE REGIMENTS.

BUT there was no lack of magnificent military material. It is certain that no state in the Union offered finer specimens of manhood for the volunteer army than did Alabama. And the examining surgeons weeded out those who were in the least defective. An index to the rigidity of the physical examinations was furnished by the rejection of men who had been known in their respective localities as athletes of more than ordinary merit. Wrestlers and boxers were rejected with as little ceremony as were men of puny stature. A man might show great muscular power but unless his physique indicated a capacity for sustained effort, unless his vital organs were unimpaired, he was not accepted. Endurance and faultless organisms were required. Eugene McElroy, of the Bessemer Rifles, was rejected despite the fact that he had a wide reputation as a heavy-weight prize fighter.

The eagerness of men to serve their country was proved by the grief that rejection caused them. It was a common scene for a rejected volunteer to lie sobbing bitterly in his tent. Unaccepted men walked from the surgeons' headquarters with tear-stained faces distorted by poignant sorrow. The affecting adieus told the accepted soldiers by those returning home afforded a powerful inspiration for the men remaining in camp. The regret of ineligible comrades over their inability to accompany them gave to the volunteers an exalted conception of their position and steeled them to bear with commendable fortitude the hardships that came afterward.

Still, the extremely rigid examinations delayed the muster proceedings. There were not enough surgeons to expedite the work. Companies were not lined up for physical inspection until their rolls showed the required quota. The delays thus occasioned lost a number of recruits who gave way to the discontent that came to them in those days of suspense. These losses perturbed the officers. Moreover, the mustering officer's announcement that the men awaiting muster would be subsisted only six days by the federal authorities, made it appear unwise to send any more troops to Mobile until the men already there could be disposed of. This advice was telegraphed to R. F. Ligon, adjutant general of the state, on May 3. It deferred the arrival in camp of several companies whose strength was meanwhile depleted by the loss of men who became impatient during the delay.

An authorized statement was given out for Governor Johnston at that time as follows: "It will be seen that Alabama is sending in her troops more rapidly than the government can receive and care for them. The governor informs the secretary of war that he has sent Alabama troops to the point designated by him; that he had no request that any part of the quota should be delayed and that he will expect the government to care for them until mustered in. The governor thinks when the president informed him how many troops he desired assembled at Mobile, if he did not want them at once, notice should have been given him. The governor has no apprehension but that the troops will be properly cared for."

Pressure was brought to bear and, as a consequence, the volunteer regimental surgeons were sworn in to aid the regular examiners. Arrangement was made, also, for the subsistence on government rations of those volunteers who were forced to remain in camp more than six days before their muster could be accomplished. Some of the volunteers were in Camp Johnston three weeks before their companies took the oath of service.

* * * * * * * * * *

Companies K, L and G of the First Regiment, were mustered in, May 9, 1898, at 11 a. m. Company A was to have gone through the exercise at the same time but the commander, Captain Parkes, had not been accepted, and his men declined to take the oath unless he were allowed to lead them. Companies K, L and G assembled under a clump of trees in the north end of Camp Clark. Each man had already signed the muster roll. Solemnly, with an earnestness that impressed the spectators as prophetic, the soldiers uncovered and, with their right hands aloft, bowed their heads in assent to the oath as read by the mustering officer, Lieutenant Hollis: "I do solemnly swear that I will bear true faith and allegiance to the United States of America, and I will serve them honestly and faithfully against all their enemies whomsoever; and that I will obey the orders of the President of the United States and the orders of the officers appointed over me, according to the rules and articles of war."

Soldiers and spectators cheered alike enthusiastically at the close of the ceremony; and the mustered volunteers returned proudly to their quarters, exultant over the fact that they were the first men in the state to go through the exercise. Captain Parkes and his company were mustered the next day. On all sides, there was an eagerness to hasten through the formalities necessary to make the volunteers "full-fledged soldiers." It was set forth to the men that if they were mustered in time, they would be paid their first wages in the early part of the following month. Moreover, it was pointed out that the sooner the oath of service was taken, the sooner the men would receive their allowance of clothes and equipage.

In the First Alabama, the examining surgeons and the

mustering officer prosecuted their work with expedition. The physical examinations of Colonel Higdon's regiment, which commenced May 3, were completed in ten days, the surgeons turning their attention to the Second Alabama on May 13. The Warrior Guards were the first company of Colonel Cox's command to undergo the examiners' scrutiny. Of the 103 men who applied for enlistment under Captain Brandon, just twenty-three were rejected, the company being left with precisely the number of accepted men required for muster.

Meanwhile the muster work in the First Alabama had progressed with such rapidity that only three companies of Colonel Higdon's command remained to be sworn, the Bessemer Rifles having taken the oath on May 11 and the Etowah Rifles, the Anniston Rifles, the Joe Johnston Rifles and the Huntsville Rifles on May 13. The Oxford Rifles were mustered, May 14, and the Wheeler Rifles, May 17. Then followed an interval of a week in which strenuous efforts were made to secure the few recruits remaining necessary to accomplish the muster of the Clark or Bowie Rifles. Recruiting officers were dispatched to Northern Alabama and advertisements were circulated for volunteers.

But the difficulties which beset the Second Alabama at that period were incalculably more embarrassing. Up to May 11, there were only eight companies in Camp Johnston. On that day, however, the Mobile Cadets and the Lomax Rifles reported for duty. Five days later, May 15, the Eufaula Rifles arrived. It was not until that day that Captain Brandon succeeded in having his company, the Warrior Guards, mustered. At the conclusion of the ceremony, the captain, a gifted orator, made his men a stirring speech. He reminded them that they composed the first company in the Second Alabama to be mustered and he hoped they would be first in everything else pertaining to the regimental history. He referred also to the Guards' proud record and concluded with an eloquent appeal to the men's patriotism. The scene of enthusiasm that followed only tended to intensify the envy of the unmustered soldiers in other companies and to aggravate their restlessness.

Up to that time, four other companies had been examined by the surgeons—the Montgomery Greys, the Montgomery True Blues, the Phoenix City Rifles and the Troy Rifles. But rejections so depleted the strength of the last three companies that they were forced to send out recruiting officers. The Montgomery Greys, however, passed the surgical examiners with a sufficient number of accepted volunteers to be mustered on May 18.

* * * * * * *

The difficulty experienced in obtaining recruits and the disposition of volunteers to become disgusted over the distressing delay prompted the officers of the Second to resort to a system of transfers similar to that by which the First Alabama had expedited its muster proceedings. Men were discussing their liability to punishment for deserting before they took the oath of service. Volunteers, who concluded that the government was so neglectful it did not deserve patriotic services at that time, urged a right to leave camp and return home. Others who were not yet discouraged argued that the men, who accepted rations on the representation that they intended to enlist and afterward refused to do so, were guilty of obtaining goods on false pretenses. In the end, however, no one was punished who deserted before taking the oath of service.

At all events it was considered necessary to muster the men in order to hold them in camp. Therefore, as soon as a company approached its quota of accepted men it was loaned a sufficient number of volunteers to pass muster. These loaned men messed, tented and drilled with the company with which they had entered camp. But their names were carried on the muster roll of the borrowing company and so long as this condition continued it was necessary for them to draw their pay and equipments with the latter command. Of course, this plan occasioned considerable confusion and an immense amount of clerical work; but there was urgent need for its adoption.

By means of this transfer method, the Gulf City Guards were mustered in May 21, and the Phoenix City Rifles, May 23. But for more than a week there had been grave and perplexing doubt as to the whereabouts of the Second Regiment's twelfth company. The Eufaula Rifles' arrival in Camp Johnston on May 16 had given the Second its eleventh company but Colonel Cox and his officers were much exercised as to what provision the governor could make for the command still lacking. The state executive had steadfastly refused to accept any company which could not offer the stipulated quota of eighty men. A captain at Vernon and another at Greenville had each offered fifty men, but in vain. The Alexander City Rifles and the national guard company at Fort Deposit were also willing to serve, but they could not raise sufficient men. The volunteers at those points were eager to go only if they would be permitted to retain their respective company organizations.

While this speculation was rife, the two regiments rivaled each other's industry in the quest for individual recruits. Already there had grown up a friendly spirit of contest between the two commands. But on the search for recruits, each volunteer felt he had material beside sentimental ends to serve. Every man strove to hasten the muster of his own regiment. In this way, circumstances arose bordering at once on the stern and the ludricous. A writer for a Mobile paper at that time attempted to describe a common scene at Frascati as follows:

"Scene at Camps Clark-Johnston:—Half a dozen travel-stained, bewhiskered Alabama farmers with carpet-bags in hand alight from the electric car. Immediately they are espied by Colonel Higdon and staff. At the same time, Colonel Cox and staff, who are watching the car station through field glasses, in the haze of evening atmosphere, read upon the carpet-bags the unmistakable sign 'Recruit.' In both camps the long roll is beat, and all of the men arise and shout 'Recruits, recruits!' Emissaries are sent out from each camp to greet the new arrivals. The farmers look on in bewilderment at the array of white tents and gorgeous uniforms. 'You want to go to Camp Clark,' says one detachment. 'Oh, no, you are looking for Colonel Cox,' exclaims the sergeant who represents Camp Johnston. There is a pitched battle in words and pantomime, at the end of which the emissaries from both regiments return triumphantly to either camp with a 'split delegation,' a compromise having been arrived at whereby the recruits are divided between Colonels Higdon and Cox."

* * * * * * *

In those days of suspense, a sort of frenzy was communicated to the waiting volunteers by the trains that passed their camps over the Louisville & Nashville Railroad. The track extended alongside of the kitchens. The whistle of a locomotive, a glimpse of blue or brown in one of the approaching car windows, a shout of "Soldiers!" and in another instant both regiments were crowded along the track. Happy soldiers, bound for the front, waved their hats at the envious volunteers huddled along the road and the latter waved Godspeed in turn. Each train with soldier passengers added to the impatience of the Alabamians. Afterward, when a flotilla of transports steamed out across the bay to the ocean beyond, bearing a division of "regulars" to Tampa, the disappointment of the volunteers who remained behind became exasperating.

In those days, too, the Alabama regiments' rank and file commenced to learn how far they were from a condition available for active service. Most of the enlisted men had supposed that a few weeks would prepare the recruits for the severest tasks of campaigning; and most of the volunteer officers had shared this belief. But the palpably indifferent results that accrued from more than a month of arduous drilling showed the eager patriots how much they were mistaken. Before the men left Camps Clark and Johnston they realized that they were not yet "fit to fight."

It was during that period, too, that the organization of the First Alabama showed its superior advantages. At a meeting of the non-commissioned officers of the First on May 13, 1898, Maj. Tom O. Smith instructed the non-coms to acquaint themselves at once with those details of military training that would render them efficient on the firing or skirmish line. In furtherance of these instructions, Sergt. Major Leon Schwarz posted a notice on his bulletin board directing the various first sergeants to visit as frequently as possible the camps of the regular soldiers in the vicinity of Mobile. The sergeant major of the First Regiment, himself, set the example of studying the "regulars" in camp and gaining from these studies a comprehensive fund of practical military information which the state had neglected to give its militia. Unfortunately for Colonel Cox's regiment, this lead was not followed by those in authority at Camp Johnston.

The difference in results was shown in a short time. In the First Regiment a police sergeant was detailed to take charge of the camp's cleanliness. D. D. McClung, of Company M, was appointed to this position. There was thus a means of fixing the responsibility for violations of the sanitary rules. In the Second Regiment the police work was done by fatigue details under non-commissioned officers assigned from day to day. The latter's duties on these details were regarded as drudgery and were discharged in a careless fashion. The fact that the work was classed as "fatigue" seemed to the non-coms of the Second to rob it of possibilities of credit.

Failure to arouse the enlisted men's ambitions was responsible for other shortcomings in Colonel Cox's regiment. Little or no recognition was given service. William B. Kramer, of Company E, and Charles Faber, of Company D, were told that they ranked as engineer sergeants and that they should superintend a system of drainage for Camp Johnston. Both were competent, but no emolument attached to the unconfirmed appointments and both found that the work embroiled them in embarrassments because no pain was taken to give them warrant of rank or exemption from other duty. After a time, they ceased to act as "engineer sergeants." Theirs was one of many instances in which it seemed that plans were made and abandoned with puerile capriciousness and whimsicality.

* * * * * * * * * *

The men were deeply concerned over the character of the equipments scheduled for them. Stories of the Spanish army's formidability with the Mauser gun rendered the volunteers eager for the Krag-Jorgensen rifle. They learned to entertain a contempt for the old Springfield rifle with which the militia had been armed. At the same time that they speculated on the ordnance designed for them, they continued to subsist largely on contributions of food and comforts forwarded from different parts of the state. Birmingham sent whole carloads of provisions to the First Regiment and the Louisville & Nashville Railroad transported these contributions free of charge.

Tuscaloosa sent the Warrior Guards generous quantities of "good things"; Montgomery shipped edibles to the two companies bearing her name; and Eufaula and Troy sent to the volunteers from their town a number of donations. But all this time the tardiness with which recruits reached camp and the inconveniences thrust upon the volunteers already there continued. So urgent became the need for additional men that various recruiting schemes were devised. Captain Robinson of the Mobile Rifles, Second Alabama, proposed to the four aspirants for a lieutenancy then vacant in the company that the one who secured the largest number of recruits should get the office. The proposition was accepted but the arrangement was never consummated.

In those days the two regiments dubbed each other "Higdon's Hoboes" and "Cox's Army."

CHAPTER V.

MUSTERING IN.

A letter by Capt. G. P. Barr, of Company G, Second Alabama, to the Eufaula *Daily Times*, under date of May 27, gives an inkling of the situation at that time. The following extract shows that even then the difference between the "regulars" and volunteers was apparent; that the better care taken of enlisted men by competent officers was reflected in the superiority of the regular army men's condition over the volunteers' plight:

"Regarding the fare of the regulars it is, as stated by your correspondent, 'all right.' They have not only the substantial food which we get, but all the season's delicacies, which they secure by disposing economically of the rations issued, too plentifully, by Uncle Sam and exchanging them for these delicacies. One company is not only faring well but has something like $1,500 surplus in the treasury obtained in this manner. I mention this merely as an example of the liberal quantity issued each company, and that we, too, will in time fare just as well under proper management, and we are blessed in this particular in having a quartermaster that's also all right.

"Health in camp is especially good considering the number here. Today I made a trip to the hospital and found only two confined therein, out of about 850 located here.

"The water we get, though somewhat warm, is absolutely pure. This, in a large measure, contributes to the health of the camp. In this connection, we wish to express appreciation and extend sincere thanks to Miss Belle Oppen-

1st Lieut. Leon Schwarz,
Battalion Adjutant, First Regiment Ala. Vols.

heimer and the people of Eufaula who so kindly furnished the 'wherewith' to buy ice. Quite a number are also indebted to Miss Mary Ellen Vaughan for smoking tobacco.

"As to the supposed coming disbandment of this, the Second Regiment, the statement is merely a surmise on the part of your informant and absolutely unfounded. Only 150 men are needed to complete the regiment and recruits are arriving daily. In case Company G is not filled by volunteers from Eufaula, her quota will be supplied by other companies here. While we much prefer having the company composed of men from Eufaula and vicinity, if we don't get them there, we will have them from elsewhere."

Captain Barr's prophecy that the volunteers would, after a time, fare as well as the "regulars," was never realized in the Alabama regiments. Officers were lacking to exercise the required judgment and économy, to teach the enlisted men how best to serve their own material interests, to inspect the kitchens and scrutinize the quartermaster's stores, in short, "to take care of their men."

* * * * *· * * * * *

There were many circumstances during the Alabama regiments' encampment in and near Mobile that, overlooked at the time, afterward became subjects of thoughtful consideration. The first religious service conducted for the benefit of Alabama volunteers was held, Sunday, May 8, in the rear of Colonel Higdon's headquarters. Chaplain Fitzsimmons of the First Regiment led in prayer and chose for the text of his sermon, a verse from Nehemiah, "They had a mind to work." Companies of both regiments were marched to the place of devotion and a large gathering of citizens attended the divine exercises.

A week later, the Young Men's Christian Association established its army tents in Camps Clark and Johnston. Newspapers, magazines, stationery and pens and ink were furnished the volunteers. Song services were held at these tents in the evenings; and frequently, soldiers, moved by emotion, would feelingly address comrades on the good derived from purity of mind and deed. Those were affecting incidents and did much to uplift and hallow the volunteers' lot.

At the same time, several lying sensationalists contrived to circulate a report that women visiting the camps were subject to insult. Fully two weeks elapsed before the ladies of Mobile became convinced of the shameful mendacity of these stories and there were some women who never did develop sufficient temerity to enjoy the hospitality of the camps. Of course, this condition of affairs was in no small way discouraging to the large element of gentlemanly fellows to whom female society would have been as much a source of strength as were the delicacies their friends sent them. But there were in Mobile a number of noble women who were never deterred from the path that their kindly hearts selected; and the names of many of them were inscribed in golden letters on the grateful memories of hundreds of volunteers.

Probably none of these women accomplished as much good among the Alabama soldiers as Mrs. Harvey E. Jones. Having two sons in the Second Alabama—members of the Mobile Cadets—she took a deep and loving interest first in that company and afterward in both regiments, supplying food and underclothing out of her own purse to distressed and needy recruits. Ice was furnished to the Y. M. C. A. tents and fresh milk to the soldiers' hospital. As the distress among the recruits from the rural districts became evident, a relief much more extensive than one person could afford was rendered necessary. At a meeting of the Mobile Chapter, Daughters of the Confederacy, on May 13, 1898, Mrs. Jones proposed that active measures be taken to relieve and care for the sons of Confederate veterans enlisted in the volunteer regiments. From the fact that many of Mrs. Jones' coadjutors were not Daughters of the Confederacy, it was thought best to organize a separate relief association, having, however, the countenance and support of every Daughter. With the aid of the Ann T. Hunter Auxiliary of the United Confederate Veterans and a number of disinterested ladies, this was done, the Ladies' Soldiers' Relief Association being formed with Mrs. Jones at the head. Intelligent and earnest assistance was rendered her by Mesdames Thomas, Levy, Richard Sheridan, E. W. Christian, E. B. Vaughan, S. Elder and James K. Glennon; Miss Amante Semmes and a number of others whose names, unfortunately, are not furnished the historian.

Contributions of money and clothing were received, no systematic solicitation being made, and the organized relief was extended to all the needful volunteers in and around Mobile. Contracts for ice, milk and buttermilk were made; men were clothed and cared for and the sick and convalescent were tenderly looked after. In a number of instances, transportation was furnished convalescing soldiers to their homes and they were started off with a hearty "God bless you" and a box of savory lunch. Sick soldiers were taken to the homes of gentle women and nursed back to health with motherly tenderness.

* * * * * * *

The first "dress" parade given by Alabama volunteers was that of the First Regiment on May 10. The Second Alabama had a similar drill on May 15, but at that time Colonel Cox's command consisted of only ten companies. The designation of commands by letters and their assignment to battalions occupied more attention in the Second than in the First Regiment, as all of Colonel Higdon's companies, save two, retained their national guard characterizations. In Colonel Cox's command, ten companies having been drafted from two militia regiments and the other two being volunteer organizations, there was a conflict of company letters; and the designations were in several cases decided by tossing coins.

The companies of the First Alabama were for the second time assigned to battalions on May 22, 1898. Their order was subsequently changed, but under the arrangement of May 22, they were placed as follows:

First Battalion, Maj. Tom O. Smith—Company A, Woodlawn Light Infantry; Company G, Jefferson Volunteers; Company K, Birmingham Rifles; Company L, Huey Guards.

Second Battalion, Maj. D. D. McLeod—Company D, Anniston Rifles; Company H, Bessemer Rifles; Company I, Calhoun Rifles; Company M, Bowie Volunteers.

Third Battalion, Maj. O. Kyle—Company B, Wheeler Rifles; Company C, Etowah Rifles; Company E, Joe Johnston Rifles; Company F, Monte Sano Light Guards or Huntsville Rifles.

It was on May 22, also, that the First Alabama's first regular regimental inspection took place.

At the parade of the Second Regiment on May 15, orders were read confirming the appointments of Lieut. J. R. Vidmer as regimental adjutant; W. E. Mickle as regimental quartermaster; and Dr. J. N. McLain as assistant surgeon. Afterward, E. Thurston Bonham, of the Montgomery Greys, was selected as sergeant major, a number of non-commissioned officers having been given an opportunity to show their relative fitness for the position. Before Lieutenant Vidmer assumed the regimental adjutancy, Lieut. V. M. Elmore, of the Montgomery True Blues, discharged the duties of that office and showed himself so familiar with affairs military that none was surprised when, several months later, a major general described him as one of the most efficient and brilliantly promising line officers in the volunteer army.

* * * * * * * *

The delay attending the muster of the various companies

prompted speculation as to the time from which the volunteers' pay would commence. Word was received from the paymaster general on May 20 announcing that enlisted men would be paid from the time of their enrolment, or the day on which they started for the rendezvous. Of course, this applied only to those who were accepted for service. It was intended to pay the commissioned officers only from their respective dates of muster. This caused deep dissatisfaction in official circles and on May 24, the following resolution was adopted, copies being mailed to senators and congressmen and the heads of departments at Washington:

Whereas, it has been made known that no provision has been made for the payment of the commissioned officers of the volunteer service in the United States Army for time spent by such officers in recruiting and equipping the troops in such service, prior to the time said officers are mustered in regularly, notwithstanding their commissions may antedate the time of their muster by several days or weeks, and they have done several weeks' work as such officers; and whereas, it is the concensus of opinion among such officers of the First Alabama Volunteer Infantry, U. S. A , that the government ought to pay for such service just as if said officers had been regularly mustered in before the cause was rendered; therefore,

Resolved, That each of the senators and representatives from the State of Alabama at Washington be requested by each of said commissioned officers to do all he can honorably to have the law so amended that such officers may receive pay for such service as if the same had been rendered after being mustered in.

Afterward, the officers of the Second Alabama signified their approval of this resolution and supported it in personal letters.

* * * * * * * * * *

One of the first boards of inquiry appointed in the volunteer army exonerated Captain H. B. Kennedy of the First Alabama on May 19, 1898, from charges preferred by Private Smith Fuller of the Huey Guards. Fuller claimed that Captain Kennedy, while serving as officer of the day on May 18, struck him with his sword during a raid on a gaming crowd.

The First Alabama was officially recognized by the War Department on May 22, a telegraphic order reaching Colonel Higdon on that day to report to General Coppinger, at the Spring Hill camp, nine miles from Frascati. But the regiment could not report until it had been mustered in. Nevertheless, it was not to be furnished uniforms or ordnance until it reached Spring Hill.

Finally, on May 24, the First Alabama was rejoiced by the arrival of a batch of recruits sufficient in number to enable Company M to muster. On the same day Capt. W. J. Vaiden solved the problem of Colonel Cox's twelfth company by escorting a command of volunteers into Camp Johnston. His company was for awhile erroneously mentioned as the Pelham Guards.

Immediately after the last company of the First Alabama went through the muster ceremony, Colonel Higdon and his staff took the oath of military allegiance. Beside the colonel, these were sworn: J. B. McDonald (U. S. A.), lieutenant colonel; E. D. Johnston, adjutant, Birmingham; R. M. Fletcher, Jr., quartermaster, Huntsville; W. J. Kernachan, surgeon, Florence; L. C. Morris, assistant surgeon, Birmingham; Hardee Johnston, assistant surgeon, Birmingham; O. P. Fitzsimmons, chaplain, Birmingham; Leon Schwarz, sergeant-major, Birmingham; Lee Joseph, quartermaster sergeant, Birmingham; D. W. Gass, hospital steward, Birmingham; R. E. Hogan, hospital steward, Birmingham.

Before that day, however, the national authorities had been prevailed upon to accept the Alabama regiments on the basis of the state's national guard plans of organization—with three majors instead of two and with three battalion adjutants as part of the field personnel. Capt. Osceola Kyle, of the Joe Johnston Rifles, was appointed the third major of the First Regiment on May 17, and Capt. W. W. Brandon, of the Warrior Guards, was commissioned third major of the Second Alabama on May 18. The three battalion adjutants of the First Alabama were appointed on May 24.

* * * * * * *

The following morning, May 25, Colonel Higdon's regiment broke camp at 8 o'clock. It was the first time the volunteers had heard the general call—the signal to lower tents—and the entire Second Regiment gathered just inside its lines to witness the abandonment of Camp Clark. Like a flash, the white canvas village disappeared. Every tent dropped at the call; and in five minutes Camp Louis V. Clark was a thing of the past.

Colonel Higdon's regiment marched through the quarters of the Second Alabama to St. Stephens' road and thence to Spring Hill, the men of Colonel Cox's command lining up on either side of the regimental street to bid them farewell. It was a notable fact that though officers of the Second signaled frantically to their men to "give the boys of the First a good send-off," little enthusiasm was evinced by Colonel Cox's regiment. Colonel Higdon's command showed plainly the results of the examining surgeons' pruning process—it was a superb body of hardy men, but its ragged appearance, the dearth of uniforms, had a dampening effect on the ardor of the watching volunteers.

Still, the men of the First were hopeful that their transfer to Spring Hill meant an early move to the front and they were enthusiastic. Encumbered with but few equipments, the regiment made the march to Spring Hill in easy fashion, reaching there at 1:30 o'clock in the afternoon. A brief thunder shower that descended while the men were en route was accepted as grateful refreshment from the heat.

On the day that the First Alabama abandoned Camp Clark, only five companies of the Second Regiment had been mustered. Colonel Cox at once redoubled his efforts to recruit his regiment to the requisite number. Posters were distributed throughout Southern Alabama and additional recruiting agents sent out. May 27, the Troy Rifles and the Jackson County Volunteers were mustered. The following day the Mobile Rifle Company was sworn in. The Eufaula Rifles took the oath on May 31 and the Mobile Cadets were mustered June 2. Five days later, Captain Vaiden's company borrowed enough men to pass muster. Then came a week of waiting and suspense. The Lomax Rifles remained to be mustered and it was found more difficult to secure the seventy men then required to fill out the regiment than it had been to get 200 recruits one month before. But on June 14 the Lomax Rifles passed muster and in the afternoon of that day the Second Alabama Volunteer Infantry assembled on the parade ground of Camp Joseph F. Johnston, underwent a verification of its muster rolls and formally became a part of the volunteer army.

CHAPTER VI.

AT SPRING HILL.

COMPETENT testimony shows that, on June 14, no regiment in the volunteer army excelled the First or Second Alabama in point of physical perfection. Colonel Higdon's men at Spring Hill and Colonel Cox's command at Frascati were constantly the subjects of admiration. Regular army men, accustomed to the spectacle of robust, hardy troops, were struck with the extraordinarily rugged appearance of both Alabama regiments. It is certain that no finer body of volunteer infantry, of equal numerical strength, had ever been collected in the western hemisphere—the domain of physical superiority.

It was natural that this should be the case. Of the patriots who offered themselves for service in Alabama, less than sixty per cent. were accepted. The examining surgeons had remained inflexible in their observance of a high standard of physical eligibility. Properly trained, either regiment—as composed in early June—could have developed an endurance surpassed by no command in the American forces, volunteer or regular.

But on May 25, 1898, the second call for citizen soldiers was issued; and it was arranged that Alabama's additional quota of white volunteers should be attached to the two regiments already formed. The plan provided for an increase of the regimental strength from 960 to 1,240, each company being raised from eighty to 103 enlisted men. The officers' commissions had been already confirmed and delivered, those of the First being dated April 30 and those of the Second, May 1, the former thus ranking the latter by one day's seniority. Their positions assured then, officers ceased to regard the matter of recruiting with that anxiety which it had occasioned them up to the muster.

Under general corps orders, issued June 6, however, recruiting officers and agents were appointed for the First Alabama, June 7, to get sufficient men to raise the regiment to the increased requirement. These appointes were: First Battalion—Capt. G. F. Hart, Sergt. E. M. Gibson, Corporal J. G. Johns and Privates Percy W. Terry and Peter H. Hambright; Second Battalion—Lieut. B. R. Field, Sergt. A. N. McLeod, Sergt. G. J. Huffman, Sergt. Joe Hodo and Private W. B. Glover; Third Battalion—Lieut. M. N. Pride, Sergt. J. H. McCoy, Privates J. H. Hannah, J. J. Challen and W. Christiensen. Recruiting stations for the First were established at Birmingham, Anniston and Decatur.

Afterward, similar appointments were made in the Second Regiment, as follows: At Montgomery, Capt. C. A. Anderson, Lieut. J. T. Bullen, Sergt. R. F. Trimble, Corporal F. C. Sagendorf, Privates J. R. Williams and H. C. Rogers; at Mobile, Lieuts. C. W. Moore, T. F. McKay and Daniel McNeill, Sergts. W. A. McCreary and J. R. Eagon, Corporal W. V. Jackson, Privates W. H. Reynolds, G. W. Otis and W. B. Kramer; at Tuscaloosa, Lieut. J. Levine, Privates Ed. E. Cox and H. F. Fairless; at Eufaula, Capt. J. R. Barr, Corporal L. Cohen and Private Ed. Sercy; at Troy, Lieut. W. E. Andrews, Corporal George W. Newman and Private W. J. Jackson; at Scottsboro, Lieut. J. R. Campbell, Privates Clare Humphrey and A. B. Parks; at Jasper, Lieut. Edgar Hayes and Corporals Jackson and Cunningham; at Phoenix City, Capt. J. P. Marchant, Corporal J. B. Wood and Private W. S. Hill; at Selma, Capt W. L. Pitts, Corporal Origen Sibley and Private G. J. Belt.

Recruits were not eager to enlist and instructions had been issued to make less exacting the standard of physical requisites. It was decided to make the minimum weight of eligible volunteers 110 pounds and the minimum height five feet, two inches. Thus, several men who had been rejected in the regular examinations were accepted at the recruiting stations.

* * * * * *

On June 15, Colonel Cox having telegraphed to the War Department that his regiment was mustered in, he was ordered to report to the officer in command at Spring Hill, for assignment to duty with the Fourth Army Corps. Three days before this order was received, Quartermaster Mickle commenced the distribution of ordnance and clothing to the Second Regiment. Springfield rifles, of the same pattern as those used by the militia, were furnished. Haversacks, cartridge belts, plates, cups and knives were also given out, but most of the articles were second-hand, having been previously in use in a regular army regiment. A limited number of canteens fell to the lot of the First Battalion.

On the same day that the regiment was assigned to the Fourth Army Corps, Governor Johnston announced his appointment of the Second Alabama's battalion adjutants, as follows: First Battalion, C. C. Hare, of Auburn; Second Battalion, Sherwood Bonner, a sergeant of Company C; Third Battalion, W. Y. Johnston, First Sergeant of Company G. But Lieutenant Hollis, the mustering officer, refused to muster the battalion adjutants or the additional majors of the Alabama regiments on the ground that he had not been authorized to do so. In the First Regiment these officers at once assumed the duties of their new positions as did also Major Brandon, but the battalion adjutants of the Second Alabama, fearful that their commissions might not be confirmed, did not relinquish their sergeancies and continued as enlisted men.

On June 16, Colonel Cox, in accordance with instructions from Washington, reported personally to Brigadier General Schwan, in command of the camp at Spring Hill, for further orders. The colonel was directed to report with his regiment the following day. Additional clothing was at once issued the Second Alabama and on the afternoon of June 16 the men were for the first time attired in heavy marching order so that they might be inspected and instructed as to the regulation method of carrying their arms and accouterments. On the same afternoon, they received their first issue of army shoes.

Camp Joseph F. Johnston was struck the next morning at 7 o'clock. The Mobile Rifles served as color company for the day. The regiment marched up the shell road skirting Mobile Bay through the city to Spring Hill, the circuitous route being somewhat longer than that traversed by the First Alabama three weeks before. Few of the men were fitted for the exertion. Their only army training up to that time consisted of drills without arms. They were unaccustomed to the heavy brogans that chafed their feet and weighted them down. The heat was unusually intense. But the regiment showed its pluck and made the march without complaint. Many staggered and faltered but courageous tenacity bore them on. Spring Hill was reached in less than four hours. There were several cases of incipient insolation and a number of the men's feet were lacerated or swollen by the brogans which, however, in after days proved a boon to them. By retreat that evening the Second Alabama was regularly installed as part of the Second Brigade of the First Division of the Fourth Army Corps at Spring Hill in the camp popularly, but improperly known as Coppinger.

* * * * * *

The drills at Frascati had consumed one hour in the morning and one hour in the afternoon. At Spring Hill, the morning drill was increased to two hours. The camp was laid in an extensive forest of pines so remote from a view of civil habitations that there the Alabama regiments received their first accurate impressions of campaign duty.

Doubt as to what programme was intended for the troops lent credence to the innumerable rumors that gained currency in camp gossip. Startling stories of immediate movements were told and retold hundreds of times each day. Deep interest was taken by the Alabamians in reports that Brig. Gen. W. C. Oates, of their state, would be assigned to a brigade ultimately composed of one Texas and the two white Alabama regiments. General Oates visited Mobile in the middle of June and was greeted with considerable enthusiasm by the men of both Colonel Higdon's and Colonel Cox's commands.

Before that time, however, the uncertainty of the War Department's plans was manifested in a most disagreeable fashion. On the morning of June 13, 1898, orders were received at Mobile to transfer the volunteer troops in that vicinity to Mount Vernon Barracks, thirty miles north on the Mobile & Birmingham Railroad. At midnight, these orders were countermanded, an immense amount of work having been done in the meantime to hasten the movement. No explanation was made, though at the time the projected transfer to Mount Vernon was attributed to a desire on the part of the Washington authorities to protect the volunteers from the danger of fever infection.

* * * * * * *

When the Second Alabama reached Spring Hill, the division encamped there, and of which Brigadier General Theodore Schwan was in command, was made up as follows:

First Brigade—First Texas, First Louisiana, First Alabama.

Second Brigade—Second Texas, Second Louisiana.

Gen. Lloyd Wheaton was in command of the First Brigade and Gen. W. W. Gordon, of Savannah, Ga., had charge of the Second Brigade to which the Second Alabama was assigned.

The condition of the troops at Spring Hill at that time is in a measure told in the following clipping from the Mobile *Register* of June 11, 1898:

"An officer at the headquarters of the division said yesterday: 'The only thing that could possibly lead to an impression that the movement of the troops from Mobile is contemplated is the fact the War Department is urging upon the division that the equipment of the men be hurried forward. And this, too, in the face of the fact that the equipment supplies are not here yet.'

"This matter of equipment, by the way, is getting to be a very vexing one, and in private conversation the government is roundly scored by volunteer officers on account of the dilatory methods employed in issuing clothing, rifles and accouterments to the men. The supplies furnished thus far, they say, have been of a very inferior quality, although the men would be content if there were sufficient to go around.

"As an illustration of the inferiority of supplies a prominent surgeon said yesterday that notwithstanding a large special appropriation was made for the purpose the government had supplied the surgeons with surgical instruments that were obsolete fifty years ago. This, he said, was without exaggeration, and the instruments were evidently cast off stock of manufacturers. The writer was also shown cartridge belts provided by the government that did not look like they cost five cents each. The leather was patched and so rotten that it could be punctured with the little finger of the hand. The sewing was crudely done with cotton thread and the cartridge webbing was sewed irrespective of any size or shape of the cartridge to be carried. Of one dozen of these belts furnished a company, no two buckles were alike. It must be borne in mind, too, that these cartridge belts were brand new and were evidently just from the manufacturer. It was said that it had been reported to the quartermaster general that they were unfit for use."

* * * * * * * * * *

On June 20, 1898, word was received that the First Division of the Fourth Army Corps had been ordered to Miami, Fla. To those who remembered that the place had been described by Gen. J. F. Wade as unfit for camp purposes, the order came both as a shock and a surprise. But a majority of the volunteers looked forward to the movement with delight. They knew Miami, Fla., was on the coast, quite close to Cuba—it was "near the front"; and the men were overjoyed at the prospect of soon seeing active service.

The drills assumed a new interest. The volunteers were eager to perfect themselves in the practice of arms; and though there were many discouraging circumstances, though it became in a measure apparent to the men themselves that their lack of training and equipment rendered them practically unserviceable against disciplined troops, the great, unbounded self-confidence of the American patriot made them eager for battle.

The First Texas Volunteer Infantry received its first payment from the government on June 22, and was immediately afterward loaded on the trains that bore them to Miami. The following day, the First Alabama, the First Louisiana, the Second Texas and the Second Louisiana were paid, the enlisted men receiving wages from the dates of their enrolment and the commissioned officers being paid only from the time of their muster in. The volunteers had been without money for nearly two months and their first pay day provoked a monstrous saturnalia. A numerous provost guard found it impossible to maintain order. Discipline was forgotten. Hundreds of drunken soldiers ran riot in the streets of Mobile, indulging in countless brawls and making the air hideous with unbridled ribaldry. Of course, there were hundreds of other volunteers who remained sober and orderly, but the orgies of the culprits in the latter part of June, 1898, afterward tended to restrict the liberties of the entire division, particularly the Second Brigade. A vacant building at the corner of Commerce and Conti streets in Mobile was converted into a temporary guardhouse and scores of offenders were thrust into it. Mad with liquor, crazed by the novel excitements which surrounded them, the imprisoned soldiers and those of their intoxicated companions who were yet at large made of Mobile a veritable Babel. On the morning of June 24, 1898, more than 400 men were absent without leave, from one of the regiments at Spring Hill.

On June 23, the First Louisiana left for Miami and the next day the First Alabama and General Schwan and his staff followed. The train bearing the Alabamians passed through Mobile, the various sections remaining long enough in the union station to permit the men to bid the assembled throngs farewell. The advance guard, on the first section, left "Camp Coppinger" at 10 a. m. The next section, bearing the first six companies of soldiers, reached the union station at 2:30 p. m. The troops left earlier than the published programme had announced, but the Ladies' Soldiers' Relief Association provided an abundance of tasteful lunches and delicacies for those aboard the train.

Brigadier General Gordon remained at Spring Hill in command of his brigade. At noon of that day the soldiers confined in the guardhouse in Mobile made a desperate effort to escape. Captain Camp of Company B, Second Alabama, was in charge. The prisoners shattered the windows, hurled bricks at the guardsmen and made violent efforts to tear the building down. For awhile, the situation was serious. But word was sent to Lieutenant Russell of the auxiliary cruiser Powhatan, then in port, and he landed a squad of ten marines who marched to the guardhouse with a number of hand-cuffs and irons which were fastened on

1st LIEUT. SHERWOOD BONNER.
BATTALION ADJUTANT, SECOND REGIMENT ALA. VOLS.

PHOTO BY LIVINGSTON, MONTGOMERY.

the more violent prisoners. Meanwhile, several citizens were struck with bricks thrown by inmates of the guardhouse. The culprits had torn up the flooring of the building and thus obtained their missiles.

In the struggles to handcuff some of the prisoners, several ugly gashes and cuts were inflicted; and altogether the day was one of the most exciting in the lives of those who were on provost guard at the time.

CHAPTER VII.

FROM MOBILE TO MIAMI.

THE same day that witnessed the departure of Colonel Higdon's regiment for Miami marked one of the most impressive incidents in the history of the Second Alabama. Late in the afternoon of June 24, 1898, a number of Mobile women presented to the Second Regiment Alabama Volunteers a flag and a deed of gift for a set of band instruments. The banner itself was not ready on that day and the company flag of the Warrior Guards was used as a substitute for the presentation. The flag committee, appointed several weeks before by Mrs. Harvey E. Jones, was composed of Misses Nellie Harrison, Amante Semmes, Grace Hopkins, Annie Prince, Lovie Glennon and Florence Glennon. Miss Semmes, a grand-daughter of the famous Raphael Semmes, was selected to present the flag; but the Clara Schumann Club, which, aided by the St. Cecelia Chorus, provided the band instruments, had delegated Misses Daisy Tacon, Eoline Russell, Lovie Glennon and Waldover to represent it. Misses Grace Hopkins, Maribel Williams and Annie Prince officiated as maids of honor for Miss Semmes.

The regiment was drawn up in close order in a hollow square facing to the inside. In the center stood a bench for the speakers. The gathering dusk deepened the shadows of the surrounding forest. It was difficult to disguise the seriousness that moved many to pretend gaiety. The troops were going to the front, everyone thought, and, in a few days, that flag fluttering in the center might wave over a bloody field strewn with the bodies of kinsmen and friends. The feelings that swayed the assemblage were reflected in the words of the speakers—words such as no other scene or circumstance could have prompted.

"We of the South have always been proud of our heroes," Miss Semmes said. "Is there in all this broad land of ours one heart that does not beat high at the mention of Washington—of Lee?   *   *   *   And even when the end had come, and Lee laid down his sword at Appomatox, and our Bonnie Blue Banner was folded reverently and laid silently, sadly away, its glorious story told its noble drama, played out to the end for long, weary years of doubt and mistrust. We were still a divided nation, and the term United States seemed but an empty sound, a hollow mockery; for the pride, the arrogance of conquest on one side, the bitterness of defeat on the other, kept far asunder the hearts of the North and the South. In that war, brother had fought against brother, father against son, and it was hard to forgive, harder still to forget. But now that is past forever. The throbbing wound is healed and once again, in very truth, we are a united people. When the call for volunteers rang through the land, from North and South alike, the answer rose: 'We come,' and side by side, against a foreign and an alien foe, the victors and the vanquished, the boys in blue and the boys in grey, forgetting that they were ever foes, remembering only that they are friends and brothers, are fighting for one cause, in one uniform and under one flag.

"Into your keeping we give your country's flag. Guard it well, because it is your country's and, therefore, sacred, and let it be to you, each and every one, a symbol of honor and truth, valor and patriotism and all other virtues; and so we will show to the world that American manhood is the highest type of manhood and the American nation is second to none. May your flag, consecrated by our love and prayers, lead you on from triumph unto triumph and may its silken folds and glorious colors shine afar, high above the dust and smoke of battle, a harbinger of victory, a rainbow on the cloud of war."

Major Brandon received the flag and in his response, too, rang Southern pride mingled with Southern loyalty. "Tell me of Grecian courage and Roman valor, tell me of the daring Stuart or the dauntless Forrest, but chivalry never had a truer representative than the loved Semmes, Mobile's own distinguished soldier," he said ; and in the next breath welled up a paean of tribute to the flag which the Confederate hero had fought. "Telegraphic wires link the hearts of every soldier, from the humblest private to the most distinguished officer, and whenever a current thrills along the line, whether of joy or grief, whether of victory or defeat, it touches a note of harmony in every breast. And so, today, fellow soldiers, as the bright eyes of the women of our fair Southland look into ours, and their lips bid us Godspeed in our well-nigh holy cause, and with their tender hands place into ours this flag, we kneel in spirit and swear that it shall wave only in victory. But, Miss Semmes, while I cannot wreathe for you and the ladies who have presented to us this flag, a garland all radiant with the flowers of poesy and rhetoric, I can come, in a soldier's plain, blunt way, and say thank you, and in this assertion I voice the sentiments of every soldier here, and, ere long, Cuba will be heard to sing the 'Star-Spangled Banner, in triumph doth wave o'er the land of the free and the home of the brave.'"

Gen. J. W. Whiting introduced Miss Daisy Tacon, who presented in behalf of the Clara Schumann Club the deed of gift to the set of band instruments. Capt. E. M. Robinson responded and in his well-rounded sentences was clearly conveyed the spirit of patriotic reunion that bound the soldiers of every section in one common comradeship under Alabama's standard. "Take back to the ladies of Mobile," he said to the fair donors, "our grateful acknowledgments with the confident assurance that every soldier's heart among us goes out to them in affectionate appreciation. Bear to them, from us, the faithful promise that the regiment which they have honored will return from this momentous conflict like the historic Spartan patriot, either 'with their shields or upon them.' Tell them for us, that whether in the Everglades of Florida, on the fruit-laden shores of Porto Rico or on Cuba's burning plains, the memory of their kindnesses will quicken the pulses of courage and awaken anew the fires of patriotic fervor. Tell them that in the gloomy dungeon or on the fields of fame—in blood-washed trenches or on towering parapets of glory—the men who today have greeted you with chivalric and enthusiastic cheers will rend the blue skies that bend above the 'Gem of the Antilles' with the joyous shouts of victory achieved; until the soul-stirring strains of 'Dixie,' mingling with the martial music of 'Yankee Doodle,' and drifting on into the majestic melody of 'The Star Spangled Banner,' echoing and re-echoing from Mantanzas, Santiago and Havana shall proudly proclaim to a waiting world that Spanish infamy has been punished, the heaven-blest cause of humanity has triumphed and oppressed and bleeding Cuba is, at least, forever free."

As a fitting punctuation to the unique ceremony, the band struck up "Dixie," and 1,000 enthusiastic throats yelled themselves hoarse.

* * * * * * * * * *

The Second Texas Volunteer Infantry left for Miami on June 25. It was Saturday—the last week day remaining before the departure of the Second Alabama; and many of the men of that regiment were eager to dispose of personal matters preparatory to what might prove their last leave-taking. Hundreds of them lived in or near the Gulf City and they were eager to transact business of moment to themselves and their families. Up to that time they had experienced the utmost laxity of discipline. The regiment had not received any wages. The muster having taken place subsequent to the close of the previous month, the pay rolls for May had not been submitted in time for liquidation in June. Many of the men had already been without funds for six or seven weeks and a visit to Mobile on that last week day meant to them much of personal importance.

But Brig. Gen. W. W. Gordon, who had assumed command of the Second Brigade only a few days before, intervened. He forbade the issuance of any passes. No one could go to town, he declared. Consternation resulted in the Second Alabama. Fervent appeals were made by men who ordinarily had no favors to seek. One man showed that if he were not permitted to visit Mobile that day, he would suffer a pecuniary loss of several hundred dollars. Others presented equally urgent requests for leaves of absence. But General Gordon was obdurate. Unofficially, the explanation was made that he with-held passes because of the scenes and doings of disorder in Mobile during the previous two days.

No consideration was given the fact that the Second Alabama had not been party to these riotous incidents; that, being still unpaid, the regiment was entitled to more opportunities for procuring personal conveniences than were the more fortunate commands; and that, withal, innocent and unoffending soldiers were being punished for the mischievousness of others. Officers were denied the privilege of issuing leaves to reliable men. The officers themselves were required not to leave camp. The enlisted men, observing the indignity with which the commanding general treated their superiors, grew to think less than ever of the volunteers' shoulder straps.

That was the Second Alabama's first experience with the querulousness and inconsiderateness of Brig. Gen. W. W. Gordon. The next day, Sunday, passes were issued—after the material opportunities offered by week-day transactions had been lost to the men who begged them.

The Second Louisiana left for Miami that day.

* * * * * * *

Grief strove with jubilance for mastery at Spring Hill that Sunday afternoon. Hundreds of men, women and children visited the volunteers' camp to bid the soldiers farewell—some perhaps forever. Mothers and sons wept on each other's shoulders; fathers spoke solemnly and sternly; brothers and sisters wrung tearful adieus.

The preparations for departure had been in progress in the Second Alabama for several days. Some time before, inquiry was made by the War Department as to the number of men in the First Division of the Fourth Army Corps who were considered immune to yellow fever. The Second Alabama reported that sixty-five per cent. of its members claimed to be immunes. The First Alabama made report of nearly as large a percentage. This inquiry, together with the fact that 7,500 ball cartridges had been issued to each first sergeant, led the rank and file to believe Miami would be the point of their embarkation for Cuba or Porto Rico. This belief gave jubilance to the volunteers and grief to their relatives. And the same idea, communicated to the public, intensified the interest that attracted crowds of spectators to the camp on the morning of June 27—the time set for the Second Alabama's departure.

There was much disappointment in the regiment over the fact that the railroad arrangements precluded an opportunity for their friends to bid them farewell in the union station at Mobile. Not only was the Second Alabama denied the means of passing through the city where thousands of friends and relatives had assembled to meet them, but a ridiculously roundabout route was chosen for them via Columbus, Miss., and Tuscaloosa, Ala., over the Mobile & Ohio Railroad to Montgomery. The other regiments had been sent through Mobile, but the Second Alabama, a great number of whose members had relatives living in and near the Gulf City, were sent over the out-of-the-way route. This circumstance, which engendered a good deal of ill-feeling in Southern Alabama, was due to a misunderstanding between Capt. F. W. Cole, chief quartermaster for the First Division, and some of the officials of the Louisville & Nashville Railroad. The direct road to Miami was over the Louisville & Nashville via River Junction and if the regiment had been sent that way, it would have reached Jacksonville earlier than it arrived at Montgomery.

The unnecessary fatigues and inconveniences, thus imposed on the Second Alabama by the absurd addition of several hundred miles to its itinerary, were afterward attributed to a lack of friendliness on the part of Captain Cole for the Louisville & Nashville, but his effort to punish that corporation resulted only in a severe punishment of the soldiers. Captain Cole had taken advantage of a technical deviation from its contract by the Louisville & Nashville and sought to use the Second Alabama as a cat's-paw with which to scratch the railroad. The unpleasantness accruing to the volunteers from this arbitrary course was accentuated at Montgomery where they were again prevented from seeing a host of friends and relatives who had gathered there at the Louisville & Nashville's union station to tell them good-bye. The Mobile & Ohio had no contract at the time with the Louisville & Nashville and the latter, naturally, did not see fit to extend to its rival the use of its union station in Montgomery and to thus, by enhancing the conveniences afforded by the carrying line, increase its own discomfiture.

Because an army official saw fit to vent what afterward assumed the complexion of partisan spleen, the six companies from Mobile and the Alabama capital were denied the comfort of seeing their home towns for what might have been to many of the men the last time.

* * * * * * * * *

But the benevolent women of Mobile did not permit this incident to undo their kindly plans. A number of the departing soldiers' relatives reached Spring Hill in time to bid the volunteers farewell. A brisk rain descended while the regiment was waiting to board the cars, and the gloominess of the inclement weather added to the melancholy of the parting scenes. Sobbing women confided their sons, brothers and husbands to the care of their officers; and every captain in the regiment was begged to assume a temporary fatherhood over scores of men. The Ladies' Soldiers' Relief Association lent to the departure an abundance of good cheer. A special train was furnished by the Mobile & Ohio railroad to enable a delegation of Mobilians to intercept the departing regiment at Whistler. A store of sandwiches and toothsome lunches was piled on the special baggage car. At Whistler the edibles were distributed among the soldiers. Each of the other five regiments of the First Division of the Fourth Army Corps also received generous supplies of cold lunches when they passed through Mobile. These comforting contributions came from a number of motherly women, few of whom received adequate appreciation of their innumerable deeds of kindliness to the volunteers. Mrs. Electra Semmes Colston, one of the foremost women in this work of charity, explained that the credit for the inauguration of the lunch distributions among the departing soldiers belonged to Mrs. William H. Ross and that she was diligently assisted in the work by Mesdames William Mastin, I. G. Thomas, and Richard Sheridan. Among the others who helped to distribute good cheer among the Second Alabama were: Mesdames J. K. Glennon, Christian, Gaynor, Gazzam and Vaughan; Misses Amante Semmes, Mordecai, Harrison, Boone, Glennon, Hopkins, Thomas, Hughes, Wheeler, Berney, Tacon, Vidmer, Middleton, Partridge, Rencher, Brewer and Cameron.

But to none was more credit due than Mrs. Harvey E. Jones, whose industry in behalf of the volunteers' comfort never relaxed. Even after the departure of the troops from Mobile, Mrs. Jones and her gentle co-workers continued their labors among the sick soldiers left behind at the Marine Hospital. To far off Miami and, afterward, Jacksonville, the loving thoughts and considerateness of these women followed the soldier boys. Pajamas, shirts, sheets, pillow-cases, underclothing and numerous other useful articles were sent to Chaplain Harte for the hospital. Money was also sent him to purchase delicacies for the sick; and he was instructed to call on the Ladies' Soldiers' Relief Association for anything of service that could be forwarded to him. The innumerable kindnesses of Mrs. Jones to the soldiers were emulated by many other Mobile women, but various circumstances contributed to blazon her in both Alabama regiments as a ministering angel. Col. Harvey E. Jones, her husband, was probably more widely known among the Alabama troops than any other Mobilian, and the scores of letters that he received from Confederate veterans and other friends begging him to "look after" their boys in different companies, were turned over to his wife; and before the two regiments left Spring Hill her personal acquaintance had extended to every company in the two commands.

* * * * * * * * * * *

The trip to Miami was a sequence of hearty receptions. The volunteers were elated. The cordiality of the towns en route made the soldiers' lot appear for the nonce much better than the government's inconsiderateness had rendered it. Fruits and sandwiches were tossed into the trains at dozens of stations. Each regiment's transportation facilities consisted of three sections composing in the aggregate thirty-two cars and coaches. The first sections, composed of fourteen cars each, bore the advance guard in charge of the stock and equipage. The following sections each carried thirteen coaches alloted to six companies and a Pullman coach for the officers.

Five days' travel rations were furnished the men but the lavish donations en route afforded ample and much more tasteful subsistence. The trains made moderate progress and the soldiers seemed to regard the trip as a prodigiously pleasant excursion. At one place in Georgia, men on one of the Second Alabama's sections climbed through the car windows and innocently raided a neighboring watermelon patch while the engine was taking on water. At Fort Pierce, Fla., a committee of citizens furnished chicken and ham sandwiches, gratis. Pineapples were flung into the cars at every stopping place in Florida; and at Jensen, a citizen, Ed Coon, gave a whole carload of the luscious fruit to the soldiers. Those were merry days for the volunteers —but, then came the martyrdom of Miami.

The First Alabama reached the "Camp of Horrors" on June 26. Colonel Cox's command, the last of the division placed en route, arrived there, June 30.

CHAPTER VIII.

WHAT CIVILIANS SAW.

JOHN S. Kendall and C. A. Williams, correspondents with the First Division, Seventh Army Corps—the regiments from Texas, Louisiana and Alabama having been transferred in the latter part of June from General Coppingers's to General Lee's command—for the New Orleans *Picayune* and Houston *Post*, respectively, have furnished the subjoined personal letters. Both gentlemen shared the comforts of the officers' tents and messes or lived occasionally among the more civil surroundings of the town of Miami itself. Their views, therefore, are the impressions of men who saw but did not suffer. And then, too, as "outsiders," they were frequently debarred from cognizance of outrages and impositions that go to make up those satanic arcana classed as "regimental secrets."

But what these gentlemen write is instructive :

JACKSONVILLE, FLA., October 15, 1898.

A full story of the camp at Miami, Fla., will probably never be written. Each man knows what came under his own observation; but none of us suffered the full round of privation and disease in that place. The stories which have been printed about Montauk and the other camps in the north, where the troops from Santiago were taken after the fall of the city, were anticipated in Miami. The same inefficiency, official neglect and cruel suffering occurred at both places. But at Miami there were circumstances which made the troops specially worthy of recognition as heroes and martyrs.

They were taken there to gratify a private enterprise and to compensate a political debt. They were sent to a climate as hot and debilitating as any that American troops have been required to exist in. They were compelled to perform not once, but constantly, the evolutions that soldiers are expected to execute on the battlefield; and this, in scorching heat without water, without proper food and through a country which in wildness and ruggedness equaled, if it did not surpass, the jungles of Santiago.

Men died from the hardship of the work. It was nothing for a hundred men to fall exhausted on the stones of that jungle-land and be taken in the ambulances to linger through tedious illnesses in the hospital.

They camped in sand where every breeze whirled the dust and dirt into their food; they sweltered by day under the sun-baked tents and by night shivered in the wet wind. They drank water impregnated by the refuse of the camps and thick with unmentionable foulness. They were taken to hospitals where the chief surgeon acknowledged no authority and refused to give them the attention which their commanders demanded for them. In their illness they tossed on sheetless mattresses, tormented by flies and insects, lacking the attention of skilled nurses, inadequately supplied with medicines, half the time without ice or milk and never furnished with those dainties for which an invalid yearns, until three disinterested ladies undertook to supply them at their own expense. What wonder that they died? And those who survived—are they not entitled to the honor and affection of their fellow-countrymen? Have they not suffered as much as those whom a better fortune sent to the brief and glorious hardships of an active campaign in the enemy's country? I think they are entitled to be remembered with those other heroes who fell at San Juan and El Caney. They had a patient and uncomplaining courage which, to us, who lived among them and saw their suffering, appeared as sublime an exhibition as ever war has shown. This is the part of the story which will never be told.

I began by saying that no one of us knew the full extent

of what our men suffered. I end by saying that no one but the God of Battles knows the limit of the heroism, the patriotism, the silent devotion and the uncomplaining endurance that was wasted in that camp whose beauty so ill-accords with its pestilence-haunted history.

JOHN S. KENDALL.

* * * * * * *

HOUSTON, TEX., October 15, 1898.

Truly, no more apt term than "Southern Martyrs" could be applied to the soldiers of the First Division, Seventh Army Corps, who for seven long and weary weeks suffered all the hardships of an active campaign, notwithstanding the fact that they were in their own peaceful country and that their only enemies were an incompetent War Department and a millionaire investor whose political "pull" was proved to be so powerful as to completely overshadow and over-ride the recommendations and protests of staff officers appointed by the United States government for the purpose of protecting its interests and the interests of its army.

It is a sad commentary on this grand republic of ours that at such a time the influence of a capitalist should be considered above and beyond the reports made to the War Department by such men as Brigadier General James F. Wade, Lieut. Col. Curtis Guild, Jr., and Lieutenant Colonel Maus, the latter two of General Fitzhugh Lee's staff. Yet such was the case at Miami, Fla., the southern terminus of the Florida East Coast Railway and the southernmost point in Florida reached by a railroad.

Miami is a paradox, if there ever was one. In the immediate vicinity of the Royal Palm Hotel, where the beautiful Miami River joins its limpid waters with those of Biscayne Bay, where tropical trees, lovely as a painted picture, stir softly over lawns of velvet green, in response to the caresses of the languorous Southern breeze, where, the white-winged boats go out across the bay, between the keys, into the broad Atlantic beyond, where every live thing seems happy and glad, where, in short, "every prospect pleases and only man is vile"—there is beauty indeed, and of a kind which would warm the heart of the painter and intoxicate the senses of the lover of the artistic in art and nature.

But behind this picture there is another, a horrible, festering, repulsive, putrefying picture, like unto the whitening bones of a grinning skeleton masked by the form of a beautiful, voluptuous woman, a picture which is buried indelibly into my memory, there to remain as long as life—a picture of man's inhumanity to man, where human beings were treated like brutes and, after so long a time, debased to the level of the animal, the larger portion of their kindly instincts, their innate refinement and their respect of the Deity crushed and ground out of them by the ceaseless pressure.

As I close my eyes and look back over the events of the past five months, the impressions received on my arrival at Miami—the first newspaper correspondent to enter there—are clear and distinct. The beauty of the place appealed to me strongly and I felt satisfied with the lot which cast me there until the novelty and the glamour passed away, the scales dropped from my eyes and the real took the place of the ideal. Volunteer soldiers who had never known what it was to labor, slaved away in the broiling sun, clearing the ground—if ground it can be called—of the heavy boulders, the sharp and jagged portions of coraline rock, the palmetto scrub, the heavy logs, the wandering roots of the tropical trees and the thousand and one other obstacles which encumbered all of the region except that which had been improved by the Flagler people at the expense of millions of dollars. There had been practically no attempt made to clear the territory alloted to any of the six regiments composing the division, except that assigned to the First Texas which was the first to arrive and which was located directly on the bay shore. From this point, back toward the Everglades, stretched the First Louisiana, the First Alabama, the Second Texas, the Second Louisiana and the Second Alabama, in the order named. The natural formations, before they were disturbed by the efforts of the soldiers, bore out to the letter General Wade's statement that the place was literally a jungle, a thicket, totally unfit for occupancy by troops. As one progressed backward from the bay shore, the roughness of the ground was accentuated. The camp of the First Texas was bad to a degree, so it can readily be imagined what conditions existed in the camp occupied by Colonel Cox's men.

As soon as the extremely arduous task of getting the camps in presentable shape was gotten well under way drilling was begun. Ah, that drilling! No English prisoner, compelled for hour after hour to pursue the endless road the tread-mill presented, ever worked as hard as did those Southern volunteers at Miami during the time they were supposed to be learning how to defend their country. A two-mile walk every day over a mere path which would have been simply execrable even under ordinary circumstances, covered as it was with palmetto scrub, underbrush and sharp stones, led them to the glade which was dignified by the name of "drill ground." Here for three long hours, under the burning tropical sun, they marched and countermarched, deployed and rallied, charged and retreated, over a patch of earth the surface of which was similar to that of all the surrounding country—rough and uneven—and cruelly hard to walk upon, especially to some of the poor unfortunates who were practically shoeless, their repeated requisitions for footwear having either been neglected or ignored. And all this, too, at a time subsequent to the announcement by Secretary Alger 'to the effect that no Southern troops would be sent to the front because they were not prepared. Great God! How could they be prepared under such circumstances? Why were they tortured

BREAKING CAMP AT SPRING HILL, NEAR MOBILE, ALA.

so? The War Department had already declared its intention of reserving the Seventh Corps for a winter campaign, yet the First Division of this once great organization was drilled as it might have been drilled had there been any chance whatever of its seeing immediate service.

Over that God-forsaken road to that alleged drill ground marched the men of six regiments every day. The burning sun beat down upon them, the thick dust was in their lungs and in their nostrils, they were bathed in perspiration. Surely the Rough Riders in that never-to-be-forgotten charge of theirs, did no harder work, nor, aside from the Mauser bullets, suffered more. Yet not a man complained. Many fell out of the ranks and sought the scant shade of the trees by the roadside when human endurance was taxed to its utmost, but not a murmur came from those brave Southern men. The blood which fired the heroes of the Lost Cause was in their veins. They had enlisted to defend the flag their fathers fought—hated then, but beloved now; they hoped to meet the enemy and with that hope ever before their eyes they toiled and suffered on, bravely, unflinchingly. All honor be to them, say I!

And then, after a few days of this sort of life, the men who had been so full of health and life and vitality at Mobile, began to sicken and to die. They might possibly have withstood the ravages of the mosquitoes and the sand flies, and the fearfully hard drills and marches, had the things they put into their stomachs to build up the tissue destroyed by their labors, been of the proper character. But instead of pure, clean water, that greatest of all natural invigorators, they were given a poisonous, polluted fluid which has since been unhesitatingly condemned by the experts of the Smithsonian Institute and by Dr. Archinard and Prof. Metz of New Orleans. This water was supposed to have its origin in pure springs back in the Everglades. The agents of the man who owned Miami said that this was the case and the chief surgeon of the division corroborated their statements. Day after day the medical officers of the various regiments reported that such was not true—that the water came from surface wells, the juxtaposition of which to the sinks blasted in the porous earth, showed beyond the shadow of a doubt that their output was not what it should be.

And, finally, this chief surgeon who had claimed all along that there was nothing wrong with the water supply and that the enormous percentage of illness was not unusual, realized the danger of his position, saw whither his neglect, his incompetency was leading him while he bestowed his smiles on the loungers at the Royal Palm hotel; and called a halt—when it was too late. The horse had been stolen, the damage done, the seeds of disease planted in the systems of those unfortunate men, there to thrive and flourish even after they were removed from that pest hole in which they were held so long.

An effort, which was partially successful, was made to improve the water supply. No benefit was realized from this, however, until a few days before the division was removed from Miami to Jacksonville, so the good done was practically nil.

Right here I wish to go on record as denouncing as the veriest rot the statements which have been made to the effect that the sickness at Miami was the result of indiscretions on the part of the men themselves—that they ate and drank things which they should not have allowed to have gone into their systems. The fallacy of this belief is proven conclusively by the fact that, although they had the same opportunities to eat and drink the same objectionable matter at Mobile and Jacksonville, and improved these opportunities to the utmost, the percentage of illness at the two camps last named was never over two per cent. Another denial of the statement mentioned above lies in the fact that for a time at Miami the percentage of illness was much larger among the officers than among the men, notwithstanding the fact that the former did not gorge themselves with unripe fruit, citric acid, whiskey and other objectionable refreshments, as the latter are alleged to have done.

The division hospital in which the sick men were supposed to be accommodated was by no means what it should have been. With accomodations for only 200 it at one time contained as many as 314. The attendance given the sick was not at all what might have been arranged had the proper attention been paid to this feature; and frequently the food furnished was of a very inferior quality and poorly cooked; and until Mrs. W. W. Gordon, the estimable wife of the commander of the Second Brigade, conceived the idea of establishing a convalescent hospital, men were frequently sent back to their companies when they should have been made comfortable and given the best sort of attention. The Red Cross Society did what it could, but in that God-forsaken hole even this powerful and far-reaching organization was unable to secure ice and milk for the sick in anything like sufficient quantities.

I venture the assertion that, had it not been for the Southern press, backed up, of course, by the proper sort of pressure, the First Division of the Seventh Army Corps would not have been rescued from Miami until the six regiments were entirely invalided. It was a hard fight and a long fight, but right and justice triumphed over greed and oppression and the volunteers were removed to the healthful camp at Jacksonville.

War in its worst forms is horrible, but in its worst forms it would hardly entail more suffering than did incompetence and neglect and ignorance and indifference at Miami, "sad Miami by the sea."

C. Arthur Williams.

CHAPTER IX.

HOSPITAL HORRORS.

MIAMI'S miseries were labeled in the regimental dispensaries. The division hospital contained only the horrors that could not be hidden inside the camps. But in the history of the medical department of the Second Alabama is told the story of sufferings revealed nowhere else. Major Kernachan and his staff encountered as many obstacles and discouragements as did Major Pugh and his assistants; but because the experiences of the latter can be written from personal observation, they are given in instance of the adversities endured by Alabamians in the volunteer service.

On May 9, 1898, the surgeons commenced work in Camp Johnston. Of the original appointes on Major Pugh's staff, Dr. G. C. Scott, assistant surgeon, and W. M. Mullens, chief hospital steward, were released from service in the Second, the latter accepting a more lucrative position in the Third Alabama.

At Camp Johnston, the surgeons found that the most prevalent ailments were catarrhal affections (colds) and diarrhœa, due to exposure or, rather, the volunteers' change from domestic customs to camp life. The scarcity of shelter and clothing was also largely responsible for this illness. When a mild case of small-pox developed in the Montgomery Greys, the surgeons endeavored to have every man vaccinated who could not show a vaccination mark. They were deeply chagrined over the volunteers' prejudice against this method of prevention, a few of the soldiers deserting rather than submit to the vaccine inoculation.

Mumps also appeared at Camp Johnston and clung to the two Alabama regiments with fluctuating virulence to the end.

The pure water at Mobile enabled the surgeons to eradicate typhoid fever in its primary infection there. Two cases of this dread disease developed at Camp Johnston in the Troy Rifles. The patients were sent to the Marine Hospital at Mobile and the disinfecting process was carried into effect in their vacated tents. Typhoid fever did not again assert itself until the regiment reached Miami.

At Spring Hill, the surgeons had expected to receive full supplies of drugs, dressings and surgical instruments. They were shown, with much military formality, a large collection of medical stores. They were also given a new medical manual and instructed to fill out requisitions for anything they needed. The division hospital steward, with very long, drooping moustaches, promised to fill these requisitions promptly. The surgical cases, litters, desks, chairs, tables, horses, saddles, pans, buckets and other hospital adjuncts to which the regiment was entitled, were "just out," it was explained, "but would be furnished in time."

The order for needed drugs was given; and it came back to the regimental dispensary with only one-half or one-fourth of some of the articles required, while other medicines were stricken off the list altogether, the long-moustached steward sending the verbal explanation that the chests containing them were not yet open. This procedure was repeatedly gone through. Afterward, it was explained that the drugs had been packed for shipment to Miami and would be delivered to the regimental dispensaries there.

Orders were received from Chief Surgeon Appel that all patients should be sent to the division hospital. The Second Alabama's sick were at once transferred in compliance with these instructions, but the two most serious cases were immediately returned to the regiment with the message, by word of mouth, that the division hospital had no time to bother with them.

One of these, W. E. Rollins, of Company G, applied at the regimental dispensary of the Second Alabama for treatment on the morning of June 27—just before the departure for Miami—and a diagnosis showed that his temperature registered at 104°. The hospital ambulance passed on its regular tour shortly afterward and he was placed in it so that he might make the trip to Florida in the hospital train. But he was again returned to the regiment with the explanation that he could not be taken care of on the hospital train.

Major Pugh indited a protest against this action. It was submitted to Colonel Cox and approved by him and Rollins was returned with it to the division hospital authorities. He claimed that he was again ordered back to his regiment which was just boarding the cars for Miami. Compelled to travel for three days and nights on a crowded, stuffy train, his health became so much impaired by fever that he afterward fell an easy victim to typhoid at Miami and died.

* * * * * * * * * *

The increasing ordeals of the soldiers involved growing tribulations for the regimental surgeons. The difficulty of obtaining medicines for the Second Alabama's dispensary continued. The arrogance of the long-moustached steward was unabated. Such absolute necessities as quinine and calomel were obtained for a time from sources other than the division dispensary.

Surgeon Pugh's repeated remonstrances were in vain. Finally, the gravity of the situation impelled him to adopt drastic measures. Preparing a requisition in the form of a forceful communication, he disregarded the dilatory process of sending it through military channels and forwarded it direct to the commanding general. Having observed that his previous protests had been pigeon-holed, he decided to pursue this method and thus bring the matter to a finality. His inability to obtain necessary medicines was set forth together with the fact that, after being in the service more than two months, he was yet without a single surgical instrument, the government having failed to supply him with even so much as a pair of forceps to extract a tooth or a lancet to open a boil. Requisition after requisition had been submitted for these things, he wrote, but without avail. There was considerable talk, at the division's medical headquarters, of a court-martial in connection with the Second Alabama's surgeon, but the needed drugs and a case of surgical instruments reached Major Pugh without further requisition. This result, however, did not accrue until Major Pugh's complaint, or protest, had been sent back with the indorsement of Major Appel, the division's chief surgeon, saying: "Wants exaggerated; requisitions not properly made out." Major Pugh promptly returned the document with this counter indorsement: "Requisitions made in exact compliance with instructions from Medical Manual and of the chief surgeon of the division and were never filled until this document was sent in; wants not exaggerated—not fully stated; facts are worse in this case than exaggerations."

* * * * * * *

Sickness continued to increase until not half the men in the regiment could be considered well; and at the same time the surgical staff was crippled by illness. At this juncture, it became necessary to assign Dr. G. A. Sheldon, a contract surgeon, to the Second Alabama. During all this time, notwithstanding repeated requests from Major Pugh, the chief surgeon never visited the Second Alabama's camp. He sharply censured the regimental surgeons for the extent of their sick lists and insinuated, as far as his official position and license made it safe for him to do, that the surgeons were not vigilant enough in the detection of malingerers. The diagnosis of typhoid fever, as made by the regimental surgeons of the Second Alabama and the Second Louisiana, were smiled at sarcastically. Ensconced in a luxurious couch in the Royal Palm hotel, in the midst of eminently congenial companions, with comforts and conveniences especially amplified for his enjoyment by a hostelry the excessive obsequiousness of whose every attache indicated that he was a favored guest, lolling in a tranquility almost sybaritic—it was not strange that the chief surgeon of the division was slow to acknowledge the horrors that raged in the camps a few hundred yards distant. There should have been no wonder that he discouraged adverse reports. He was loath to abandon the Eden into which he had strayed.

But ceaseless protests from the regimental surgeons and the storm of indignation that swept throughout the South had their result. Lieut. Col. L. M. Maus, chief surgeon for the Seventh Army Corps, accompanied by Lieut. Col. Curtis Guild, inspector general on Maj. Gen. Fitzhugh Lee's staff, went to Miami to investigate. As soon as the red tape—broad, red tape which had already coiled in fatal folds around many noble American boys—could be disposed of, Lieutenant Colonel Maus was shown the true condition of affairs while Lieutenant Colonel Guild inspected the men—the pale, anaemic, jaundiced, fever-racked Alabamians who, six weeks before, had formed the giant regiments of the South.

*　　*　　*　　*　　*　　*　　*

The regimental surgeons showed Lieutenant Colonel Maus abundant reason for the division's immediate removal, but the trammels of military formality withheld from him intelligence of scores of circumstances that went to make up the wretchedness, misery, agonies and torments of Miami. His investigation was made along general lines. It did not delve into the instances of individual torture that made Miami for many men worse than the unspeakable black hole of Calcutta. It did not deal with the absence of proper nourishment for the patients, of the employment of incompetent and untrained nurses.

Lieutenant Colonel Maus found that Miami's climate has a torridity equal to that of Cuba without the mollient features of mountains and cool mountain streams. He found that the camp was laid on a coraline wall that shuts the Everglades off from the ocean. The surface of this wall is covered by a stratum of sand which greedily devours the extraordinary rainfall that prevails. It seemed to those who inspected the camps that some seismic disturbance had raised the soil to an altitude fifteen or twenty feet above the sea level. The rock, torn and battered in this upheaval, lay scattered in all directions, sharp, jagged corners and points jutting up, half-covered by the dark foliage of the tropics or submitting to the tendril-like embraces of the wiry palmetto roots. This rock was undergoing a process of disintegration in which the regimental surgeons discovered an alarming development. A large element of animal or nitrogenous matter, preserved inside the rock for a period by the presence of lime, was escaping from its prison and charging the rain water that percolated from rock to soil and finally accumulated underneath the sand stratum. The water thus charged became a most energetic medium for the propogation of the *bacillus communis coli* and the *bacillus typhosus*. Afterward, an analysis showed that water furnished the volunteers was charged with these bacilli—the germs of the bowel disorders and typhoid that carried off scores of Southern martyrs and ruined the health of others.

* * * * * * *

The location of the Second Alabama's camp was more prolific of mortality than the quarters of any other regiment at Miami. Close by straggled the Miami river with its wide, marshy banks that were flooded and freed with the rise and fall of the tide. The water, semi-brackish, was of a character idealic for the abode of malaria. Major Pugh protested to the major general commanding that the Second

Alabama's camp was unfit for habitation, using as one of his arguments the fact that the rise and fall of the water in the river exposed malarial germs that menaced the health of the entire regiment. The general responded that he had investigated the matter and found the rise and fall of the tide averaged only four inches. The conversation drifted into general matters and mention was made that a little steamer had gone aground that morning in the mouth of the river. "She should have been afloat before this," the general commented, "as the water seems to have risen at least eighteen inches since she struck this morning." And he did not seem to notice the contradictoriness of his own statements.

* * * * * * *

On October 19, 1898, Dr. L. M. Maus testified before the War Investigating Committee. An Associated Press dispatch of that date had this to say:

"Dr. Maus was questioned in regard to the camp at Miami. He said he had investigated it and found it to be unsuitable on account of the water, which analysis had shown to be impure.

"Mrs. Gordon, wife of General W. W. Gordon, in relation to the hospital at Miami, sent a letter in which she made serious charges, among others one to the effect that a hospital nurse had become intoxicated and set fire to a patient's bed, burning him somewhat, and another that flies were often found crawling into the mouths of dying patients.

"Dr. Maus had a report from Dr. Vilas, in charge of the hospital, read, admitting the statement concerning the burning of a patient's bed, but denying all others. Dr. Maus expressed the opinion that the charges were exaggerated."

Dr. Alexander Kent, pastor of the People's Church at Washington, D. C., and field agent for the Red Cross Society, who went to Miami to investigate the horrors there, also gave testimony before the War Investigating Committee in October, 1898, and this extract from his deposition is apposite here: "Before the female nurses were secured, the nurses, who were men of the hospital corps, were not capable. They were not intelligent, as a class, and while some of them were doggedly faithful, they failed to meet the requirements. They did not, for instance, seem to regard it as of consequence if flies were crawling in and out of a sick man's mouth."

* * * * * * *

One scorching July afternoon, the writer, afflicted with a violent attack of fever, applied to the division hospital at Miami for treatment. Dr. Vilas, who was present, declined to receive him except on the order of his regimental surgeon. Half delirious and scarcely able to walk, he turned away; and were it not for the charity of Dr. W. H. Oates, a contract surgeon, he would have been forced to essay the trip of more than a mile in the blazing heat to his quarters. Dr. Oates arranged for his treatment and the order for his acceptance in the hospital was received from Major Pugh that evening. The incident indicated the callousness that characterized the hospital service. Dr. Oates discovered that the writer's temperature at the time was a fraction more than 104°. "A walk back to the camp right now might kill you," he remarked.

Two nights later, a typhoid fever patient in a ward adjoining that in which the writer lay, narrowly escaped cremation at the hands of a drunken nurse. Covered with bed sores, emaciated into the likeness of a skeleton by the ravages of five weeks of typhoid, the victim was scarcely able to roll out of his tent. The nurse had overturned the lamp and thus set fire to the canvas. That was the case referred to by Mrs. Gordon in her letter to the War Investigating Committee.

* * * * * * * * * *

The next night, when fever-racked patients had won uncertain repose from exhaustion, a hulking hospital steward stalked into the ward with a lantern. In a flash every patient was awake. The intruder was escorting a drunken soldier to a place of rest. One peevish patient begged that the light be extinguished. "Shut up, there!" roared the visiting steward. The complaining man, querulous with fever, struggled to his feet. The steward advanced toward him threateningly. The ward nurse tactfully interfered; but before noon, the patient who had complained of the disturbance, was jibbering in delirium.

The next day the steward, in charge of the ward in which the writer lay, became drunk. Half the patients failed to receive their medicines. Dr. Oates ordered the culprit under arrest. He was replaced by a nurse who celebrated his accession to authority by imitating his predecessor. Dr. Oates had him removed, also.

Incompetent nurses, untrained and unfitted for hospital attendance, aggravated the illnesses of patients. The writer observed the case of two typhoid fever patients who were fed oatmeal in direct violation of the attending surgeon's instructions. One of them died before the writer was sent back to his regiment. Solid food of any sort is ordinarily fatal in conjunction with typhoid—the veriest tyro at nursing is expected to know this—but there were hospital nurses at Miami better fitted for the slaughter-pen than the sick room.

* * * * * * * * * *

Such comforts as finally reached the hospital patients came from civilians. Not enough milk was available to sustain the typhoid sufferers. Men died solely because they could not be given the proper sort of nourishment. It was not until shortly before the orders arrived for a removal to Jacksonville that arrangements were perfected for the shipment of milk to Miami in refrigerator cars from St. Augustine.

There was no asylum for convalescents until Mrs. W. W.

Gordon, wife of the Second Brigade's commander, assisted by two charitable ladies, succeeded in establishing a ward for the benefit of men dismissed from the division hospital and yet too debilitated to return to duty. The Red Cross Society lent its aid; and the painstaking and indefatigable industry of the chaplains did incalculable good to sufferers who could look nowhere else for comfort. In the self-sacrificing attentions of persons unattached to the hospital service was found the only oasis in the desert of Miami martyrdom.

Major Pugh protested again and again, with ever increasing vehemence, that the men were being done to death. Surgical boards of inquiry were appointed but soi-disant martinets sought to squelch their reports. One commission, of which Major Pugh, was a member, proved that though the Miami authorities had asserted that the water furnished the regiments came from the Everglades, it was taken from the surface wells or covered cisterns instead. General Gordon advised that this report be not made. He questioned its accuracy, he said. The indignant surgeons devised a ruse to substantiate their assertion. They cut off the pipe that ostensibly led from the Everglades, but the water supply continued. Then they shut off the pipes that led from the covered cisterns; and the water supply was suspended. Thus it was proved that the entire division was drinking from the covered cisterns, most of which were tainted with seepage that had percolated through the sand and porous soil from the latrines. The board of inquiry made its report in the face of General Gordon's opposition.

* * * * * * * * * *

J. A. McDonald, manager of Mr. Flagler's Miami interests, resented Major Pugh's "officiousness." He sent a letter to Colonel Cox intimating that the Second Alabama's surgeon was too eager to find fault. Major Pugh wrote a reply, couching it in such terms that his friends became apprehensive of a duel. There really was a danger of a personal encounter. Nothing showed better the extent of bitterness to which the fight went to continue the Miami martyrdom.

* * * * * * * * * *

Meanwhile, Professor Metz, of New Orleans, announced the startling result of his analyses of samples of Miami water forwarded to him by Major Archinard of the Second Louisiana. Every week, Major Pugh submitted a formal report—like that of the regimental surgeons of the First and Second Texas and the First Alabama and Second Louisiana—declaring the systems of the men were so debilitated by hard drills, poor clothing and bad food that they offered an excellent field for the growth and spread of the disease germs that abounded on all sides. The surgeons were regularly required to explain the terrible increase of illness and that was their report.

On Wednesday, July 27, 1898, the division's sick list was as follows:

Regiments.	In Division Hospital.	In Quarters.
First Texas	52	215
First Louisiana	68	27
First Alabama	40	48
Second Texas	58	242
Second Louisiana	39	73
Second Alabama	57	128
Total	314	733

And there were twice that number of men not on the sick list but really unfit for duty. When unreasonable officers intimated that there was a great deal of malingering, they were reminded of the tremendous amount of toil the soldiers had performed in clearing the land for their camp. "Men who work like that do not malinger," the surgeons said.

* * * * * * * * * *

Commanding officers discredited the stories that Miami water was noxious or morbific. But the following official communication throws light on the situation:

HEADQUARTERS SECOND BRIGADE,
FIRST DIVISION, SEVENTH ARMY CORPS,
CAMP AT MIAMI, FLA., July, 26, 1898.

Circular No. 12.]

Regimental, battalion and company commanders will notify those detailed to boil the water for drinking and cooking purposes that it must be boiled steadily for at least one hour, in order to destroy the hurtful germs that may be in the water; and said commanders will see to it that this is done and will strictly prohibit the drinking or using for cooking any water that has not been boiled for at least one hour.

By command of Brigadier General Gordon.

RUFUS E. FOSTER, 2d Lt. 2d La. Vol. Infy.,
Acting Adjutant General.

Before that day, the death-dealing rigors of the daily routine had been so forcefully pointed out that even the lethargic compassion of General Gordon was aroused and a change was made—a change proving an absolute lack of consideration on the part of those who had charge of the Second Brigade at Miami. Conditions went from bad to worse.

On July 14, 1898, during the inspection tour of Lieutenant Colonels Maus and Guild, orders were issued changing the drill hours of the Second Brigade. Under General Order No. 15, it was required that "regimental commanders and regimental surgeons forward to the headquarters of the Second Brigade on Saturday, July 23, a report as to what effect the changes may have had upon the health of the officers and men." Up to that time the drill hours had been: 9 to 10 a. m.; 1 to 4 p. m. The change effected on July 14 embraced this routine: Reveille—first call, 4 a. m.; reveille—assembly, 4:20 a. m.; mess—coffee and hard-tack, 4:30 a. m.; drill—first call, 4:45 a. m.; drill—assembly, 5 a. m.; recall, 8 a. m.; mess—breakfast, 8:20 a. m.; sick call, 8:40 a. m.;

drill—first call, 2:50 p. m.; drill—assembly, 3 p. m.; recall, 4 p. m.

The folly of this change was shown in the increased sick list. In the First Alabama, Lieutenant Colonel McDonald had recognized that to accept these hours would be to stultify himself as an officer; and he immediately consulted Brigadier General Wheaton who assured him that so long as he was in command his men would not be robbed of repose in order to suffer additional exposure to disease. The First Brigade declined the change of hours. In the Second Alabama, Major Brandon sent a letter to General Gordon setting forth the fact that men were dying every day and that much of the terrible condition of affairs was due to the early morning drills—that "exhausted by nights of sleeplessness, the soldiers could not endure the excessive heat and terrible exercise occasioned by the new routine."

MAJ. WILLIAM W. BRANDON.
COMMDG. THIRD BATTALION, SECOND REGIMENT ALA. VOLS.

CHAPTER X.

SOLDIER SLAVES.

MR. Flagler appropriated $10,000 out of his own purse to aid in making habitable the camps at Miami. It was not from the manual labor of the volunteers that his agents expected his interests to profit. The advertisement of his health resort resulting from the presence there of a whole division of soldiers—that was the benefit his managers reckoned on.

J. R. Parrott, as Mr. Flagler's representative, approached Brigadier General Gordon with reference to the men's tents. He told the general that lumber would cheerfully be furnished to floor every tent in camp. The commanding officer of the Second Brigade of the First Division of the Seventh Army Corps, appointed to take care of nearly 4,000 men, brusquely told Mr. Parrott he had charge of the camp and would tolerate no interference. He refused the lumber for the enlisted men's tents, though the officers managed to obtain wooden floorings for their own quarters.

Mr. Parrott then went to Major General Keifer but met with no better success. The general commanding the First Division of the Seventh Army Corps was more courteous than the commander of the Second Brigade, but he was not one whit more eager to lend to the comfort of his men. Mr. Parrott was forced to abandon his mission, disgusted and sick at heart.

This episode furnishes an insight into the treatment of the men at Miami. Weeks afterward, the War Department issued general orders that in all camps where soldiers were likely to remain for any length of time, the quartermasters should issue lumber for tent-flooring. But Generals Keifer and Gordon had denied their men this comfort and hygienic protection when the material therefor could have been secured without cost to them or the government.

It was claimed that these officers sought to harden their commands for the privations of a Cuban campaign. But they subjected them to such distresses and hardships that before a month had passed at Miami, the division was more in need of tender ministrations than fitted for military duty. Exquisite torture so deadened their senses that the men did not fully realize the extent of their sufferings until a return to endurable conditions pointed out the unspeakable contrast between reasonable treatment and the handling they had received.

Every regiment in the division, save the First Texas, was forced to convert a tract of land, no more penetrable than the chapparals of Texas, into an unencumbered waste. The work was stupendous. When the Second Alabama reached the site selected for its camp, the men could scarcely believe it was intended to pitch tents. The ground was practically impassable. Field officers dismounted in order to pick their way through the palm-covered knolls, so honey-combed with jagged stones that a fall or a mis-step meant a serious accident. The walk of half a mile from the railroad depot alone involved an extraordinary exertion. Sand and dust of the fineness of pulverized borax cluttered the miserable paths to a depth varying from four to ten inches. Every step raised a stifling cloud.

* * * * * * *

The work of clearing this jungle-land was prosecuted with a vigor that proved the industry of the men. But no slaves ever toiled harder under a more terrible strain with less reward than did those American patriots, struggling with interminable palmetto roots, tugging at huge bowlders and breaking rock to ballast a land so uneven that a furrowed field were like a polished plane beside it. Then when the day's slavery had ended, came a night of mingled anguish and exhaustion. Sand flies and mosquitoes—the diabolically industrious gallinippers of the tropics—joined forces with venomous bugs to make repose impossible. Relief from myriad bites and stings was obtained only on the leeside of a brush fire where the smoke exorcised both sleep and the insects.

Weaker than when they retired, the men arose in a chilling dew for reveille. Then came the daily routine of drills and slavery, apparently devised with devilish ingenuity to destroy the last bit of remaining endurance. Two miles and more over unused wagon roads, so weighted with sand and dust that the distance seemed quadrupled, brought the men to what was intended for their drill ground. The march itself was debilitating.

At first these long, strength-stealing, brain-searing tramps were made in the afternoon, so shortly after the mess call that there was little or no opportunity to digest the almost indigestible food. It was 1 o'clock when the men left camp. Recall was ordered blown at 4. Several thousand men enveloped in dense clouds of malodorous sand and dust are uncomfortable. But when these several thousand men are encumbered with guns, marching in close order, the fierceness of the sun's heat re-enforced by an extraordinary radiation of animal warmth, every step increasing the density of the dust clouds, swarms of stinging gallinippers boring through uniforms and shirts—when men are thus tried and the torture of unquenched thirst gripes them, then the condition becomes intolerable. But American soldiers—Southern martyrs—bore these things until Death joined hands with Exhaustion and the two specters held revel in the Miami camps—the court of Official Incompetence.

* * * * * * *

There were few canteens. The government had not yet

fully equipped one-third of the men. Indeed, some of the volunteers were so poorly clothed that it became impracticable for them to drill. The scant supply of shoes soon wore out. Men went practically bare-footed. Captain Robinson, of Company E, Second Alabama, bought shirts for forty of his men at a Miami store.

But the dearth of canteens wrought more hardships than did the absence of any other article of equipment. The terrible heat was alone sufficient to cause thirst, but the severity of the marches to the "drill ground" intensified the craving for water. The dust and sand arose in such density that for minutes at a time the soldiers could not see an arm's-length ahead. In the stifling, choking darkness of these marches their thirst became excruciating.

A stagnant, noisome ditch skirted the drill ground and during the first few days the men begged permission to quench their thirst from it. But the tepid, bad-tasting dregs turned the stomach. The men did not need, after that, to be forbidden to drink from it. Wagons were ordered to haul water for the men on drill. But frequently the barrels were overturned before the wagons reached the soldiers. Seldom did they give the men relief.

* * * * * * *

On the afternoon of July 7, the Second Alabama went through its first regimental drill in extended order. Between the drill field and the Miami River lay a forest of interlacing pines and palmettos, carpeted with palm shrubs, cumbered by heavy logs and studded with the sharp, jagged rock that made the vicinage almost impassable. The men were sent charging through this forest, over a stretch of country so broken that no advance in line was possible. Tacticians witnessing these evolutions wondered at their purpose. To go scurrying helter-skelter at imminent danger of loss of life or limb, through a forest so wild that no battle save a sharp-shooters' engagement would have been possible in its confines, seemed of no avail. "It is to harden the men," the explanation was made—to harden suffering soldiers for impossible situations and improbable tasks.

Limbs were fractured. The stones cut the men's feet and tore their scant clothing. Private Henry Levinson, of Company C, suffered a compound fracture of the knee-cap; Private J. F. Grove, of the same company, had his feet severely bruised and cut; Private R. R. Denton, of Company B, was carried from the field unconscious. Then the regiment returned to the clearing in which close order movements were to be executed. Panting with fatigue, their parched tongues protruding from swollen lips, their faces livid and distorted with thirst, the men presented a pitiable spectacle. At least, they thought, there was respite for them in the approach of the water wagons. But an unmanaged method of distributing the water left one battalion unprovided for when the regiment was recalled to attention. The captain, first lieutenant and first sergeant of one of the companies of this battalion secured a filled canteen. In front of their company, every member of which was agonized by thirst, the trio drained the vessel. There were men in the ranks to whom a gulp of that water would have been medicinal—would have meant rescue from nights of throbbing fever.

This was an example of the work done by and the care taken of the men at Miami.

* * * * * * *

Then came sickness and daily deaths. A change of drill hours was tried in the Second Brigade. A sleepless night and an empty stomach did not equip the men for the ordeal. Bathed in perspiration, they were plunged into the damp foliage, saturated with the peculiarly cold dew of the tropics. The sudden immersion sickened them. The miasmatic vapors exhaled by the awaking plants quickened the work of disease and death. Recall was scheduled to sound at 8 a. m. It was frequently 9 o'clock and later when the men reached camp. Then, many were too exhaused to eat their tardy and uninviting breakfast.

Enervated, in despair and disgust, men fell into their tents reckless of what was to come. With glazed eyes and pallid faces, they lay until the swirling sand and dust, blown across them in gossamer-like sheets, mingled with their perspiration in cakes of repulsive and health-killing filth. They lacked the energy to go to their meals; and baths were unavailable. The salt water of the Miami river did not clean them and the gallinippers made bathing unpleasant.

In such extremity, the men of the Second Alabama had added to their misery the humiliation of duress. The lines of other regiments were open; not so, Colonel Cox's command. Men were denied the solace of shady nooks in the neighboring woodlands.

* * * * * * * * * *

They had become sodden in their woes. Word of Cervera's undoing and the signal triumph of American arms over Spain convinced the division that its hardships were being suffered in vain.

Disgust deepened. On July 6 a number of "kickers" in the Second Alabama succeeded in fanning into flame the regiment's disaffection. "The men want their pay," they announced. "We have been two months in the service, have cleared Flagler's land for him and we haven't received a cent." Word was secretly given that the men should refuse to respond to the drill call that afternoon. When the decisive moment came, half a dozen companies hesitated. But American reverence for constituted authority asserted itself, and, after a few moments of delay, the regiment went out to drill.

The arrival of the Second Alabama's band instruments in early July and the receipt of the regiment's colors on July 10 afforded some diversion to Colonel Cox's men. On the latter day, the regimental battle-flag was unfurled with fitting ceremony in front of the colonel's headquarters, the regiment drawn up in close order, standing uncovered, at attention. Colonel Cox opened the exercises with a brief address prefatory to the president's proclamation urging that thanks be given for the nation's recent victories. Chaplain Harte led in prayer and Rev. Dr. Neil Anderson, of Montgomery, then visiting Miami, spoke briefly. Arising after a short prayer, he concluded with a recitation of Rudyard Kipling's Recessional. "To the colors" was sounded; and the battle-flag given by women of Mobile was formally installed in the quarters of the Second Alabama.

* * * * * * * * * *

Meanwhile, an entanglement over the battalion adjutants and the third majors of the Alabama regiments made it appear doubtful that those officers would ever be mustered. But Major Brandon made a vigorous fight and triumphed. He prepared an exhaustive brief covering the legal and technical features of his appointment. The proof thus presented convinced the authorities at Washington of his right to his commission as a third major and he was mustered in at Miami, July 18. Major Brandon's case was the predicate on which battalion adjutants of both regiments established the validity of their commissions; and all of them shortly afterward formally assumed their positions. But the battalion adjutants of the First Alabama having taken up their duties as soon as they were commissioned—May 20—afterward received pay from that date.

The "unpaid Second" as Colonel Cox's regiment came to be known, found occasion for envy in the thriving canteen that contributed to the prosperity of Colonel Higdon's men. This canteen, established at Spring Hill in early June, had prospered very much. In Miami, its receipts were reliably reported to have aggregated as high as $500 on some days.

But the pall of death hovered over Miami and men became sordid, dividing their attention between speculation as to the approach of pay day and the danger of epidemic. They had already lost the spirit of aggressiveness that one month before made them tingle at the thought of battle.

An instance of the increase of suffering at Miami is given by the growth of the Second Alabama's sick list there. On June 30, when the regiment pitched camp, the sick list showed sixteen privates and no officers. July 9 there were eighty-one privates and three officers sick; July 16, ninety-two privates and six officers; July 19, 165 privates and five officers.

The paymaster came at a critical juncture. On July 20 and 21, the First Division of the Seventh Army Corps was paid in full, the officers receiving the money due them from the dates of their commissions and being thus recompensed for all the active service they had rendered.

The Second Alabama's first pay day was, of course, disquieting, but stringent regulations reduced the number of cases of disorder. It was at Miami, however, that the summary field courts, presided over in their respective regiments by Lieutenant Colonels McDonald and Thurston, tried a larger number of charges than during an equal period at any other camp.

* * * * * * *

If General Keifer's command were at that time engaged in the most hazardous campaign, the men would not have been more deeply exercised over the prospect of peril. At Miami, they shuddered at danger of death in an unfurnished hospital from a miserable malady. The entire division was thoroughly alarmed. Demoralization followed. The apprehension that prevailed, humiliating in itself, and, lacking the thrill that is the invariable concomitant of the danger of conflict, only tended to steep the men deeper in despair. Exaggerated rumors contributed to the distraction. Reports of the most unreasonable character gained currency and credence. One night, men were confused by a widely circulated story that Miami had been quarantined.

An inexplicable censorship added to the difficulty of the situation. Newspaper correspondents were instructed that in addition to being prohibited from writing anything concerning movements of troops, they would not be permitted to send out any matter derogatory to the camp. "My instructions," the censor said, "are to cut out anything calculated to discourage recruits from enlisting." An American censor appointed to deceive American patriots so that they might volunteer to serve under the American flag!

Finally, acknowledgment was made that the men had been worked beyond reason—the drills were reduced, practically abandoned.

At such a time, word was received with unbounded joy that the authorities had at last listened to the storm of protest which went up from the entire South and—decided to rescue General Keifer's division from further decimation at Miami. But to remove the men to a new camp meant to acknowledge openly the injudiciousness of having sent them to Miami. A transfer to Jacksonville could be made on the ground that it was intended to mobilize the Seventh Army Corps at that point. On July 29, General Keifer received orders to hold his troops in readiness to move. The division became delirious with delight. Song services of praise were conducted that night in the Y. M. C. A. tent of the Second Alabama. Emissaries had been sent to the camps by various Southern executives to investigate and report on the horrors of Miami. Inspector General May and Adjutant General Jumel of the Louisiana National Guard organization were among those who reached there on such a mission. The rank and file jubilantly attributed to the influences of friends at home the order for their removal.

In the camp of the Second Louisiana a bonfire was started. The entire division yelled itself hoarse. "We'll hang old Flagler to a sour apple tree," was taken up from company street to company street and echoed throughout the camp in one mighty chorus by soldiers who blamed the millionaire owner of Miami for their hardships.

The next day orders were received for General Keifer's men to move at once to Jacksonville. Captain Cole, the division quartermaster, declared that Mr. Flagler's agents were placing obstacles in the way of the troops' removal. He claimed that false reports were made of an inability to secure adequate rolling stock. His request to General Keifer for permission to seize a number of box cars then at Miami and load the men on them was seconded by offers such as that of Major Brandon, of the Second Alabama, who told the major general that, if given license, he would undertake to move his battalion in the following twenty-four hours no matter what might be the attitude of the railroads.

After some delay, the division reached Jacksonville, the Second Alabama leaving Miami on August 4 and arriving at Camp Cuba Libre—as Maj. Gen. Fitzhugh Lee's Corps quarters were known—on the next day. The First Alabama left Miami on August 12 and arrived in Jacksonville, August 13. Meanwhile, the latter regiment was notified—published report being made on August 3—that, with the Second Texas, it would be detached from the Seventh Army Corps and sent to Porto Rico. This order, however, was never confirmed, Major General Miles afterward reporting that he required no reinforcements for his Porto Rican campaign.

CHAPTER XI.

DISAFFECTION IN THE FIRST.

AN anomalous state of affairs developed at Jacksonville. Disaffection in the First Alabama gave to that regiment a retrograde tendency while confluent auspices lent to a wonderful improvement of Colonel Cox's command. The unpleasantness in the former body owed its origin to dissatisfaction on the part of a majority of the officers with the colonel. A series of disagreeable incidents started at Mobile when Captain Parkes and Lieutenant Going were notified of their arrest on the ostensible ground that they had displeased the colonel by failing to attend a social function at which he had requested all his officers to be present. Of course, nothing resulted from that affair. At Miami, Colonel Higdon and Chaplain Fitzsimmons figuratively crossed swords, the former peremptorily and, it was reported, with unwarranted surliness, refusing to give the latter a furlough. At that time Chaplain Fitzsimmons offered to leave the arbitrament of their differences to a vote of the officers of the regiment.

Friends of Colonel Higdon circulated the story that a number of his subalterns were banded together for the purpose of elevating Lieutenant Colonel McDonald to the colonelcy. Conservative men declared that this story owed its origin only to the palpable fitness for command of Lieutenant Colonel McDonald. The open rupture of the entente cordiale between Colonel Higdon and the majority of his officers came after the regiment had encamped at Jacksonville. He was accused of "prostituting his office to vent personal spleen." A memorial was verbally presented to him requesting his resignation. It was an open secret that the field officers had been deputed to present this request.

Colonel Higdon went to Birmingham on a furlough. The impression gained ground among the enlisted men that the colonel was seeking to have them mustered out and that a majority of the officers were endeavoring to thwart this purpose. When he returned from Birmingham, the rank and file gave him an enthusiastic reception while the officers remained in their tents, with but one or two exceptions. On August 31, a number of the officers prepared a set of seven charges against the colonel of the First Alabama. The receipt two days later of word that the regiment was to be mustered out prompted these officers to drop the matter. At that time it was intended to veil the affair in obscurity but, subsequently, partial disclosure was made of the circumstances that occurred in Jacksonville.

After the regiment had returned to Birmingham, an inkling of the difficulty between Colonel Higdon and his followers gained publicity through the subjoined cards printed in the *Age-Herald*. Colonel Higdon was quoted as saying that he had sought to guard the interests of the men and this card was given out in contradiction:

"HEADQUARTERS FIRST ALABAMA
"UNITED STATES VOLUNTEER INFANTRY,
"JACKSONVILLE, FLA., Sept. 1, 1898.

"We, the undersigned officers of the First Alabama United States Volunteer Infantry, now on duty at Jacksonville, Fla., do hereby state that at a meeting of the officers of this regiment, called on or about August 20, 1898, by Col. E. L. Higdon, commanding the regiment, for the purpose of considering the question as to whether the regiment wished to go intact with the Seventh Army Corps to Cuba or not, the question was asked Colonel Higdon 'if the men were to be consulted or not,' and we certify on honor that he in substance replied: 'No; they have nothing to do with it. If the officers go the men will have to go.' We are moved to make this statement because of the fact that both in private and publicly at the home headquarters of the regiment, Birmingham, Ala., Colonel Higdon has seen fit to produce the impression that factions exist among the officers of the regiment, brought about by the colonel's attitude being favorable to the men, when, in fact, as above stated, he refused to allow them a voice.

(Signed)

"J. B. McDonald, lieutenant colonel; Tom Smith, major, First Battalion; O. Kyle, major, Third Battalion; O. P. Fitzsimons, captain and chaplain; A. Harrison, captain, Company I; Thomas Hardeman, first lieutenant, Company M; B. R. Field, first lieutenant, Company D; H. C. Laughlin, captain, Company F; M. N. Pride, first lieutenant, Company E; Lawrence E. Brown, first lieutenant and adjutant, Third Battalion; R. B. Going, first lieutenant, Company G; Tom B. Cooper, first lieutenant, Company I; Henry T. Dean, second lieutenant, Company K; W. J. Parkes, captain, Company A; R. G. Mallett, second lieutenant, Company M; Thomas T. Huey, captain, Company H; E. D. Johnston, first lieutenant, Company K; Leon Schwarz, first lieutenant and adjutant, First Battalion; Robert L. Brown, first lieutenant, Company B; W. E. Wallace, captain, Company E; W. M. Martin, captain, Company B; N. G. Canning, captain, Company E; Thomas M. Hooper, second lieutenant, Company F; William A. Hasson, second lieutenant, Company C; N. D. Lacy, first lieutenant, Company L; R. M. Fletcher, Jr., first lieutenant and assistant surgeon; C. L. Ledbetter, captain, Company K; W. J. Webb, second lieutenant, Company E."

The foregoing statement was printed September 20, 1898. Then followed a rejoinder from Colonel Higdon accompanied by a statement from J. W. Moore, an enlisted man who filled a clerical position at the regimental headquarters. Some comment was caused by the fact that the enlisted man's letter was better written than the colonel's. Here is Colonel Higdon's defense:

"Camp Falkner, East Lake, Sept. 20, 1898.

"In reference to the statement made by some of the officers of the First Alabama in *The Age-Herald* this morning, I have this to say: In the first place I think it was very unkind in the officers to have such a statement printed at the present time, while I am so unwell as not to feel able to make a full statement of the facts.

"If the officers intended doing me justice they would have stated all the facts in that meeting. I called the officers together and made the statement that I had done so in order that I might know the sentiment in reference to going to Cuba as a regiment; that I wanted them to consult with the men and see how many desired to go. Some one of the officers spoke up and said it was not necessary to consult the men, but moved to take a vote then. At this point some one asked the question, 'if the men would have anything to say if this regiment was ordered to Cuba?' and I made the remark, 'that if ordered, they would all have to go; that no one would have any voice in the matter.' My intention was to convey the impression that the officers and men would have to go if ordered by the War Department. Some officers in the Third Battalion at this point spoke up and said they thought it best to postpone the meeting until they could consult the men, and I made the statement then and there that I thought the suggestion a good one, and tried to get them to adopt this plan, but the majority wanted to take a vote at this time, which I allowed them to do, and all the officers voted to go.

"The day peace was declared I went on record at that time in a conversation with Lieutenant Colonel McDonald, which I do not think he will deny, that I was now heartily in favor of all members of the First Alabama, who had left good positions and who had family ties that required their presence at home now that the war was over being allowed to return to their homes, and after the War Department made the announcement that the wishes of the men should be consulted, and after finding that a large majority wanted to return home, I did everything in my power to see that the wishes of the enlisted men were granted.

"My action toward the men before this meeting and afterwards speaks for itself, and I ask you to talk with them, as they can give you a full history of all the unpleasantness I have had with the officers and I think they will tell you that I have at all times tried to do what I thought was to the best interests of the regiment, and my action towards the men at all times is within itself sufficient to denounce as absolutely false the statement made in the headlines of your paper this morning that I would not allow the men in my regiment a voice in the matter. I have respected their wishes, and now feel proud to refer you to these 1,300 men, who feel themselves treated justly by me and who will support and substantiate my statements.

(Signed) "E. L. HIGDON."

J. W. Moore enlisted in Company K but his service at the regimental headquarters enabled him to learn a great many official secrets. Colonel Higdon therefore considered Moore a competent witness and the following letter from him was printed below the colonel's statement:

"On the day that Lieutenant Colonel McDonald asked the men for their sentiment in regard to going to Cuba I was sitting at my desk in the adjutant's office when some one came in and told me that the colonel had the regiment in line at the head of the company streets, and was going to take a vote on the question which at that time was absorbing the attention of both officers and enlisted men. I left the tent and went to where the men were forming in line. When the colonel first asked the opinion of the men I was too far away to hear the exact words in which the question was put, but did note that not a man in the regiment moved. Then again he repeated the question and I caught it, which was, 'All who want to do their duty, and go willingly to Cuba, if ordered, step three paces to the front.' This caused a move in the lines, and some went to the front. Company M, that stood directly in front of the colonel, only nine men walked out, all the balance of the company standing in their places like statues. In Company F, twelve men went to the front. I counted as fast as I could and although I could not verify the correctness of the count, yet am sure that I could not have been more than fifty out of the way in my count of 250 men who stepped to the front. The expression which came over the face of Colonel McDonald was undoubtedly one of disappointment, as he made no announcement at all at that time, as to the result of the vote, but told the men to get to their places in rank and marched them off to drill. It was late when they returned to camp that evening, consequently was after dark before the officers got their supper. But immediately after supper the colonel came into the office and asked me if any one had brought in any reports for him. I told him no, but at the same time Lieutenant Hooper, of Company F, came into the tent and when asked by Lieutenant Colonel McDonald how he found his men, he replied that he found 40 to 22 in favor of going to Cuba. This company, it will be remembered, sent but twelve men to the front in response to the vote taken by the colonel that afternoon.

"At this time Lieutenant Johnston, of Company K, came into the tent and in the presence of Colonel McDonald, Lieutenant Schwarz and Lieutenant Hooper, asked me how I stood on this matter, and I answered that like the majority of the men I wanted to go home. And inferring from the remark made by Colonel McDonald to Lieutenant Hooper, I inferred that the officers had been instructed to canvass the streets in quest of the votes of the men who were not in line at the time the vote was taken, and upon

MAJ. S. S. PUGH,
SURGEON, SECOND REGIMENT ALA. VOLS.

this supposition I asked Lieutenant Johnston if he had canvassed Company K, and he answered yes, and that he found five to two in favor of going to Cuba.

"I felt sure that he was making a false statement, and determined there and then to investigate the matter and see that Company K, of which I am a member, got justice. So I forthwith went down to the street and asked some of the men who were in the kitchen if they had been given a chance to vote, and they said no, and also asserted that there were many others who had not even been given a chance to vote. I told them to get together, and I in the meantime would secure an audience with the captain and see if our rights cannot be respected. The captain very politely allowed us an interview, and I called to the men to come up, and they came and quickly gathered about the captain's tent. I asked the captain to explain to the men the object of the vote taken to-day, and what was to be accomplished thereby, in answer to which he said that the vote simply meant nothing only to gain for the War Department the general sentiment that prevailed among the men in regard to going to Cuba. I asked him if the vote taken to-day was going to cut any figure in our going or not, and was told by him that it would not. Then I asked why so much interest was being taken by the officers in the affair if the vote was so insignificant. To this we could only get the very unsatisfactory reply that our vote was not to be taken into consideration, and that they just wanted a sentiment of the men. Then I asked if this vote was to get the sentiment of the men, why would it not be better to get the true sentiment instead of a false one, which could have been made up without bothering the men at all. He of course claimed ignorance of any false reports being made, and I have no reason for accusing him of any knowledge thereof; but in the presence of all the men I told the captain about the report brought in by Lieutenant Hooper of

Company F when our men were praising this company for their loyalty to the men. I also told him about Lieutenant Johnston giving in a report that after thoroughly canvassing Company K, he found five to two of those who were not in line in favor of going to Cuba, and told him to look around him and he would see seventeen men, besides myself, who had not been allowed to vote at all, all of whom were in favor of going home, and that if our vote did not turn out to be of interest to us, he must bear in mind that Company K was not fairly represented, and that eighteen men were not allowed a voice in the affair. He promised to see to it himself that our vote would be taken into consideration and would report it himself, which would represent Company K as having 48 to 31 in favor of going home. I dismissed the men and went back to my office, determined to see if Captain Ledbetter would fulfill his promise to the men and have our vote recorded; but it was fully an hour after the report had been formed and taken to town by Lieutenants Schwarz, Fletcher and Johnston that Captain Ledbetter came to headquarters, and I knew we had been entirely shut out.

"J. W. MOORE.

"September 20, 1898."

The following day Moore printed a card abjectly declaring that he had intended to cast no reflection in his letter on the honor, honesty or fairness of Lieut. E. D. Johnston.

CHAPTER XII.

RETURNING TO CIVILIAN LIFE.

THERE was abundant reason for felicity at Jacksonville among the two Alabama regiments. Of course, a keen solicitude prevailed concerning the Alabamians left in the division hospital at Miami, fully 100 of them having been too ill to make the trip with their comrades. But of the sick who were able to travel, a majority at once made rapid strides toward robustness at Camp Cuba Libre. Orders were issued, however, to send all convalescents to Pablo Beach, eighteen miles from Jacksonville. Inadequate arrangements at that place occasioned considerable discomfort to the men sent there. Afterward, report was made officially that the deaths of Anthony Sammereier and E. E. James, both of Company B, Second Alabama, were largely due to neglect.

But the "present for duty" men of the entire First Division of the Seventh Army Corps regained health, strength and vitality at Jacksonville with remarkable readiness. Discipline became easier of accomplishment. Officers found that sound men are much more tractable than invalids, querulous with exhaustion or fever.

The First Division's quarters—in Fairfield, a suburb of Jacksonville—were picturesque and attractive. But it was in Camp Cuba Libre, that the men of the Second learned to understand the real extent of their colonel's overzealousness. They were denied the liberties allowed other regiments and discontent was not slow in brewing. The lines of other regiments were open, but members of Colonel Cox's command were allowed to leave camp only on written passes;

and these passes were limited. Yet, with the felicitous adaptability of Americans, the men adjusted themselves to the situation, though losing none of their eagerness "to fight or go home." The Second Alabama was encamped on the west bank of the St. John's river, half a mile from the First Alabama. A description of the Alabamians' quarters, printed at that time, said:

"Visitors peeping into any of the tents are surprised at the orderly array of domestic utensils. Shoe brushes, towels, mirrors, shaving mugs and racks of every conceivable nature have been fitted into the tents until the camps have assumed the complexion of a city of canvas cottages. Throughout the regiments a settled sense of location has turned the soldiers' inclinations toward the diversions that attracted them at home."

* * * * * * *

It was then that the officers of the Second Alabama, under the guidance of Lieutenant Colonel Thurston, succeeded in writing the name of their regiment across the pages of the nation's history. There was no longer any prospect of winning glory in the clash of battle; the glamour and pomp of actual war had already fled and only the sobering quiet of an armistice remained, but the Second Alabama volunteered to relieve the government of possible embarrassment by plunging itself into the yellow fever-swept district of Santiago de Cuba. The victorious Americans then stationed there were eager to return home. Depleted in numbers by bullets and disease and debilitated by the torrid climate, they showed ample excuse for a desire to return northward. But no other troops were eager to replace them. "To fight Spaniards is one thing, but to fight yellow fever is another," volunteers said. At that juncture—on August 9—a meeting of the officers of the Second Alabama was held and it was unanimously agreed to forward to Adjutant General Corbin a telegram in effect as follows:

We, the undersigned officers of the Second Alabama Volunteer Infantry, with a majority of our command, hereby volunteer to relieve the troops now in the yellow fever-stricken district of Santiago de Cuba. We are from Mobile and Southern Alabama generally, and are about as nearly immune as any regiment in the service.

Lieutenant Colonel Thurston and Capt. W. J. Vaiden prevailed on Brigadier General Gordon to indorse on the communication his approval. He voluntarily attached the sentence, "With regret at the prospect of losing so good a regiment." Then Captain Vaiden was deputed to carry the message to Major General Lee. That officer urged the withdrawal of the offer. He argued that the regiment was destined to leave for Cuba as part of his command within a few weeks and that it would be unwise to interfere with such plans as had already been made concerning the Second Alabama. The request for transfer to Santiago was withdrawn in deference to Major General Lee's wishes.

* * * * * * * *

Deep anxiety was occasioned by the uncertainty of the War Department's plans regarding the volunteers. Major General Lee's assertion led the Alabamians to believe they would go to Cuba under his command. A large element were reluctant to experience garrison life. They had enlisted as volunteers to fight, not as "regulars to soldier." But the prospect of foreign service lent interest to affairs military. The drills—half as long as and during more reasonable hours than those at Miami—were gone through with a snap and zest. Curiosity was felt as to the scores made at the target range at Cocoa-nut Grove, six miles from Miami, whither the First Alabama and the Second Battalion of the Second had gone for practice during the encampment on Mr. Flagler's land.

Still, publication of intelligence that 100,000 volunteers were to be mustered out created a furore among the Alabamians. Word that the men would be permitted to express their wishes with relation to their term of service led a number to formulate petitions for discharge. There were some few enlisted men who, eager to do duty on foreign soil before returning home, felt disposed to continue in the volunteer army. But these numbered less than fifteen per cent. on August 15, 1898. Some of them were hopeful that they might find opportunities for unusual profit in Cuba or Porto Rico and that their service as garrison troops would end before another year passed. Fully eighty-five per cent. of the enlisted men from Alabama waited with painful anxiety for news that they were to be discharged. Orders were issued in the Second that any movement in the direction of an organized effort to be mustered out would meet with punishment.

It was at that juncture that Sergt. R. E. Austill, of Company C, Second Alabama, persisted in circulating a petition requesting the discharge from service of his regiment. Sergeant Austill had, through manifestations of a marked individuality, won considerable prominence among the enlisted men. His petition was being numerously signed when Captain Robinson, under the colonel's instructions, placed him in arrest. The following letter from Austill's father, published in the Mobile *Register*, reflects the condition of sentiment at that time:

"It was not my intention to take any further notice of the arrest of my son and the taking of his sergeant's stripes from his coat, by order of Col. Jim Wade Cox, of the Second Alabama Volunteers, at Jacksonville, but proof has come to me from every direction that the officers of our volunteer regiments have not only ignored the privates, but in many instances have punished them for daring to express their wishes or to sign petitions to be mustered out.

"As the privates are not allowed to speak for themselves, some of us who are not liable to be punished and reduced to ranks by officers, should speak for them through the public press. Does not this course of the officers lay them open to the suspicion that, because they get good salaries and have an opportunity for promotion and have comparatively an easy time, they are disposed to take advantage of the enlisted men and keep them in service after the war is over? As the officers have not allowed the privates to sign petitions representing their wishes, how can they safely say a majority of the men want to remain in service? The officers of the First Alabama Volunteers had a meeting on the 24th instant and resolved that the 'statement that a majority of the enlisted men antagonize further service is absolutely false.' They passed this resolution without calling on the men to vote. And yet, it seems that on that day 850 men of that regiment had signed petitions asking to be discharged. When it was made known that the government would muster out a large number of volunteers and would give preference to those who wanted to be discharged, the privates had just as much right as the officers to be heard and our colonels should have given them a chance and each private should have had one vote and each officer one. Remember, we are considering the rights of volunteers who volunteered to fight for their country, not to enlist as regular soldiers. The war being over, they have a moral right to be released, and I cannot see that any disgrace is to be put upon a private volunteer who would now prefer to return to his peaceful pursuits. With volunteers

> Rank is but the guinea stamp,
> The man's the man for a' that.

"I will not consider my son disgraced because Colonel Jim Wade Cox took off his sergeant's stripes. I am glad when he was arrested by Captain Ed Robinson that he had the manliness to tear off the signatures to the paper, except his own, before giving it to the captain, and that he did not seek to hide behind a round robin or to drag others into trouble. His punishment, however, is a punishment of every volunteer who dared to sign a petition and I very much doubt the necessity or wisdom of such a step.

"God bless the volunteers! They made this country free and great and will keep it so if treated with that consideration to which they are entitled.

"It is to be feared that the association of our volunteer officers with the regular army officers has put an idea in their heads that enlisted men have no rights. Lieutenant Colonel Thurston, of the Second Alabama Volunteers, is a lieutenant, I am told, in the regular army and, if report is true, he is now in Washington seeking to keep the Second Alabama Volunteers in service. Is it to be supposed that he has either consulted the wishes of the privates or that he cares a fig what they think? His position reminds one of the lines we read in Quackenboss:

> And thou, Dalhousie, thou great God of War.
> Lieutenant-Colonel to the Earl of Marr.

"I hope the governor of our state will have an opportunity to muster out both the First and Second Alabama Volunteers and let our men and officers—reduced to ranks—all come home and help to build up our great state. The Third Regiment wants to go to Cuba and it should be gratified.

"H. AUSTILL.

"Mobile, August 27, 1898."

Influences of every description were brought to bear in the fight between the friends of the officers to continue the regiments in service and the friends of the enlisted men to have them mustered out. Considerable acrimony entered into the struggle. Word that Lieutenant Colonel Thurston had gone to Washington was wired home by enlisted men; and Congressman H. D. Clayton hastened to the national capital to plead for the volunteers who desired their discharge. It was during that period that Maj. W. W. Brandon, of the Second Alabama, endeared himself to the rank and file of both regiments. Going to Montgomery, he set forth to Governor Johnston in eloquent terms the cause of Alabama's soldiers who had suffered their full share and were entitled to resume their peaceful vocations. Then, returning to Camp Cuba Libre, he was assigned to conduct the Second Alabama's summary court, in the absence of Lieutenant Colonel Thurston, but discreetly contrived during this time to advise the men as to the proper course for them to pursue. Their gratitude led them into several situations embarrassing to the major. One evening the men of the Second broke through the guard lines and, surrounding Major Brandon's tent, cheered him till they were hoarse. He advised them to return to their quarters and remain dutiful. At that moment Colonel Cox ordered the assembly call blown so that quiet might be restored. The men went trooping back good-naturedly to their company streets.

Governor Johnston had already wired Colonel Cox to take the sense of his regiment concerning continued service. The colonel protested that such a course was in violation of military ethics. He made application for permission to comply with the governor's request but it was denied at division headquarters. Nevertheless, through the energy and tactfulness of Major Brandon, Governor Johnston was fully acquainted with the men's wishes and, at the invitation of the War Department, he recommended that Alabama's white volunteers be released from service.

* * * * * * *

August 14, the Alabama regiments received their wages for July.

Proof of the excellent military material in the rank and file and of the indifferent administration of the two regiments became apparent in Jacksonville, also. As late as September 1, it was necessary to issue a general order in the Second Alabama acquainting officers with a regulation they ought to have known long before—that company commanders should be promptly notified of the confinement in the guardhouse of any of their men. Before that, at Miami, this general order was issued:

Officers confining enlisted men will prefer charges promptly where the offense is of a sufficiently serious character to warrant.

The commanding officer regrets to note dilatoriness of officers in this respect, which tends only to create contempt for the only means of discipline.

Despite this order, a non-commissioned officer of the Second Alabama was held in confinement—part of the time in the guardhouse—from July 29 to August 24 without trial. The commanding officer was himself responsible for the man's arrest. The prisoner was finally released on his captain's representation that in military law there was no warrant for holding a prisoner more than eight days without trial.

On August 31, 1898, the Seventh Army Corps paraded

through the streets of Jacksonville in celebration of the nation's victory; and no command in that body of 30,000 men presented a better appearance than the two Alabama regiments. Indeed, it was generally conceded that the Second Alabama made a showing second to no other regiment in the Corps.

Brigadier General W. W. Gordon was relieved of his command to act as a member of the Porto Rican evacuation commission; and his brigade was taken charge of by Col. L. M. Oppenheimer of the Second Texas. Before his departure, General Gordon was presented with a handsome gold watch by the officers of his brigade; and in his speech of thanks, he made reference to such "exactions as he may have imposed," explaining that he had always been eager to harden his command for the exigencies of active service.

On September 2, word was received at Jacksonville that Governor Johnston's recommendation for the muster out of the two Alabama regiments had been favorably acted on; and the enlisted men were overjoyed.

It was ordered that so soon as the preliminary arrangements could be completed, the two commands should be taken back to Alabama and released on thirty days' furlough, after which they should reassemble for muster out. The lieutenant colonels were appointed mustering officers for their respective regiments, but subsequently Lieutenant Colonel McDonald was named chief mustering officer— Lieutenant Colonel Thurston being relieved—with Capt. M. O. Hollis as his assistant for the Second and Lieut. G. W. VanDeusen, adjutant of the First Artillery, U. S. A., his assistant for the First Regiment.

But there remained a great deal of clerical work to do at Jacksonville. The transfers, made at Mobile to expedite the muster in of companies, had been set straight at Miami— by the First Alabama on its arrival there and by the Second after its first pay day—the names of the transferred men being finally installed on the rolls of the commands with which they originally volunteered. This fact complicated and increased the clerical work required on the muster out rolls. None of the men had been fully equipped and few received more than half of the regular allowance of clothing. Their accounts had to be reckoned and full report made of the ordnance issued. Afterward, it developed that on their discharge, the average payment to the privates was $76, divided as follows: Wages for September and October, $31.20; balance due on clothing account, $30; commutation of rations during furlough, $7.50; travel fare to place of enlistment, $7.50.

Both regiments were ordered to muster out at Mobile. But representation was made that most of the men of the First Alabama lived in the vicinity of Birmingham and that it would be more convenient to release them there. Colonel Higdon's regiment was then instructed to proceed to East Lake, Ala., for disbandment. Meanwhile, citizens of Montgomery succeeded in having the War Department also change its orders concerning the Second Alabama, Colonel Cox's command being instructed in the end to muster out at the state capital.

Finally, on September 16, both regiments left Jacksonville, Fla., for Alabama. The men expected a hearty welcome on their return home and, indeed, a number of enthusiastic receptions were accorded them en route. But Montgomery, which was reached early on September 17, disappointed the home-coming soldiers. No organized effort had been made to receive them. No committee met them at the depot to tell them they were welcome. Maj. Tom O. Smith's battalion of the First Alabama marched through the city and a crowd followed them back to the union station. The Second Alabama was chagrined that Montgomery, after having wrested the regiment's camp site from Mobile, did not manifest any appreciation of its success.

The First Alabama proceeded to East Lake, the city of Birmingham giving the regiment a magnificent reception. Thousands of persons lined the streets, cheering and shouting. Flowers and bunting were profusely employed for decorations; an abundance of lunches was provided for the soldiers; and the returning regiment was overwhelmed with cordial hospitality. The men were taken on the street cars to East Lake where the camp was pitched and named in honor of Col. J. M. Falkner.

The Second Regiment was switched over the railroad to Riverside Park, in Montgomery, where the men quietly pitched their tents in an unpromising tract adjoining the Fair Grounds. The camp was named in honor of Alabama's ex-Secretary of the Navy, Hilary A. Herbert. A barbecue had been arranged for the regiment by citizens of Montgomery to take place on September 21. But the authorities established a quarantine station inside the space alloted to Colonel Cox's command and protest was made that the stoppage, in such close proximity to the soldiers, of trains from the infected yellow fever districts, was a serious menace to the men's health. Indeed, Major Pugh advised that the trains be forced to move on. But the municipal authorites declined to alter the situation. The relationship between the regiment and the city thus became strained; and Colonel Cox, with some austerity, sent word to the citizens that his men would neither parade nor attend the scheduled barbecue.

The work of releasing the regiment on furlough was hastened. The ordnance was turned in to Capt. M. O. Hollis and on September 20, the men were paid their August wages and allowed to leave on thirty days' furlough. Captain W. J. Vaiden remained in charge of the camp with more than 100 men who volunteered from different companies to forego their furloughs. The Second Alabama was ordered to return to Camp Hilary A. Herbert on October 19.

The First Alabama was paid its August wages on September 19 and released on furlough on the following day, under instructions to report back on October 20. Adjutant L. C. Brown assumed charge of Camp Falkner and the men who remained there during the thirty days. But the First Alabama did not surrender its ordnance at that time.

Both regiments reassembled promptly on the days respectively appointed. In the interim, however, the malignance of the yellow fever epidemic in Louisiana and Mississippi and the consequent menace to Alabama formed the basis of a request to the War Department that an additional furlough of thirty days be granted to both regiments, the men to be notified of the extension of their leaves without returning to camp. But the War Department ordered that both commands be mustered out as soon as the processes could be gone through, while those men who happened to be in the quarantined district were excused from returning to their companies. Arrangements were made to forward to these few absentees their discharge papers and the money due them from the government.

Colonel Higdon arranged a sham battle for his command at East Lake for the benefit of the Sisters of Charity and

Hillman Hospital of Birmingham. The affair took place on October 22. Major McLeod and six companies, assisted by Battery B of Montgomery, attempted to hold a hill against Major Smith with six companies. Of course, the assaulting party triumphed and planted its colors on the crest of the hill after an exciting exhibition.

On October 23, the First Alabama turned in its ordnance to Lieutenant Van Deusen and the physical examinations for muster out were expeditiously prosecuted in both regiments under the direction of Major S. S. Pugh at East Lake and of Major Flagg, U. S. A., at Montgomery. Colonel Higdon's regiment was on parole during this period but guard lines were placed around Colonel Cox's command.

Lieutenant Colonel McDonald went to Atlanta and arranged for a sufficient number of paymasters to pay the men as soon as the work preliminary to muster out was finished. The discharge papers were dated October 31, 1898 and payments were made to that date.

Thus, the state's white volunteers returned to civilian life after just six months of army service fraught with suffering and privation but, withal, evidencing the patriotism and loyalty and the magnificent manhood of imperial Alabama.

INDEX.

	PAGE.
Argument	7-12

DEATH ROLL—
First Alabama (see addenda)	13
Second Alabama Regiment (see addenda)	14
Causes of Death	15

MEN OF THE FIRST ALABAMA—
Field and Staff Officers	16
Company K (Birmingham Rifles)	17-19
L (Huey Guards)	20-22
A (Woodlawn Light Infantry)	23-25
G (Jefferson Volunteers)	26-28
H (Bessemer Rifles)	29-30
D (Anniston Rifles)	31-32
M (Clark Rifles or Bowie Volunteers)	33-36
I (Oxford or Calhoun Rifles)	37-38
C (Etowah Rifles)	39-40
E (Joe Johnston Rifles)	41-43
F (Huntsville Rifles)	44-46
B (Wheeler Rifles)	47-49
Regimental Band	50-51

MEN OF THE SECOND ALABAMA—
Field and Staff Officers	52
Company A (Montgomery Greys)	53-55
L (Phoenix City Rifles)	56-58
F (Warrior Guards)	59-62
D (Montgomery True Blues)	63-65
E (Gulf City Guards)	66-68
M (Mobile Cadets)	69-71
B (Lomax Rifles)	72-74
C (Mobile Rifle Company)	75-77
H (Troy Rifles)	78-79
I (Jackson County Volunteers)	80-83
G (Eufaula Rifles). (see addenda)	84-85
K ("Vaiden's Rough Walkers")	86-88
Regimental Band	89-90

CHAPTER I. ASSEMBLING AT THE STATE RENDEZVOUS—
Women Retard Recruiting	91
National Guard Organization	91-92
Appointment Lieutenant Colonels	93
Volunteers Leave Birmingham	93-94
Selection State Rendezvous	95
Separate Companies Report for Duty	95
Routine of Calls	96
Camp Louis V. Clark	96
Board of Examiners (120)	97
Sergeant Collins killed	98
Small-pox Prevented	98
Second Regiment's Commander Chosen	98
Colonel Cox Names Camp Johnston	99

CHAPTER II. SOURCES OF INCOMPETENCE—
National Guard Inefficiency	100-108
Unjust Selection of Officers	100-108

INDEX.

Illegal Commissions...101-102
Merit not Title to Office...100-108
Militia Untrained...100; 103-104
Orders Ignored...105-106
Guard Duty Misinterpreted..105-106
First Superior to Second Alabama...................................106-107
Lieutenant Colonel McDonald..106-107
No Warrants Issued Second's Non-Coms...............................107-108

CHAPTER III. CAMPS CLARK AND JOHNSTON—

Change Alabama Women's Attitude...109
Presentation First Alabama's Colors................................109-112
"Camp Life in a Nutshell."..112-113
Volunteers Poorly Fed and Supplied.........................(120)..   114
Early Camp Jubilance..114
Officers Responsible for Poor Food.................................115-116
Lack of Discipline...117-118
Faithfulness Wins Hardship..117
Desertions Before Muster In...118

CHAPTER IV. RECRUITING THE REGIMENTS—

Magnificent Military Material...119
Grief of Rejected Volunteers.......................................119-120
First Companies to Muster..121-122
Difficulty of Obtaining Recruits...................................122-125
Transfer Scheme Employed...123-124
First Alabama Studies the "Regulars"....................................126
Difference in Regiments' Police Systems............................126-127
Food Contributions..127

CHAPTER V. MUSTERING IN—

Captain Barr Describes Camp Conditions.............................128-129
First Religious Services in Camp..129
Y. M. C. A. Tents..129-130
Volunteers Libeled..130
Ladies' Soldiers' Relief Ass'n—Mrs. H. E. Jones, (153-154) 130-131
First Dress Parade..131
First's Companies Assigned to Battalions................................132
Payment of Volunteers...133
First Alabama Mustered..134
Additional Majors and Battalion Adjutants............(183)   134;134
First Alabama Goes to Spring Hill.......................................135
Second Alabama Mustered...136

CHAPTER VI. AT SPRING HILL—

Physical Excellence of Alabama Volunteers...............................137
Raising the Regimental Quota.......................................137-138
Recruiting Officers and Agents..138
Second Alabama goes to Spring Hill.................................139-140
Orders to Mount Vernon Issued and Revoked...............................141
Alabamians in the Fourth Army Corps..................134; 139; 141
Equipments..142
Orders to Miami...143
First Alabama's First Pay Day...143
Soldiers' Saturnalia...143-145
First Alabama Leaves for Miami..144

CHAPTER VIII—FROM MOBILE TO MIAMI—

Presentation Second Alabama's Colors...............................146-149
Confined to Camp...149-150

INDEX.

Farewell Scenes at Spring Hill.. 151-153
Immune to Yellow Fever... 151
Ball Cartridges Issued... 151
Absurd Railroad Arrangements 151-152
Incidents en route to Miami..154-155
Arrival in Miami... 155

Chapter VIII. What Civilians Saw—

Alabamians Transferred to Seventh Army Corps............... 156
John S. Kendall's Description of Miami.....................156-158
C. Arthur Williams' View of Miami..........................158-163

Chapter IX. Hospital Horrors—

Surgeons' Views of Miami..................................164-176

Chapter X. Soldier Slaves—

Mr. Flagler's Offer.. 177
Horrors of the Miami Camp..................................178-185
Censorship... 185
"Unpaid Second"..182-183
First Alabama's Canteen.................................... 183
Second's Colors and Band Instruments 182-183
Passes Denied.. 182
Orders to Jacksonville.....................................185-186
Departure for Jacksonville................................. 186

Chapter XI. Disaffection in the First—

Officers Dissatisfied with Their Colonel....................187-188
Statement Printed by Officers...............................188-189
Colonel Higdon's Rejoinder..................................190-191
Private Moore's Defense of His Colonel......................191-194

Chapter XII. Returning to Civilian Life—

Alabamians Recover Robustness.............................. 195
Second Offers to Brave Yellow Fever........................196-197
Enlisted Men Eager to be Mustered Out......................197-201
Officers Desire Continued Service 197-201
Sergeant Austill's Reduction...............................198-201
Major Brandon's Triumphant Fight...........................200-201
Colonel Cox and Governor Johnston Disagree................. 201
Illegal Imprisonment....................................... 201
Seventh Army Corps Parade..................................201-202
Orders for Muster Out......................................202-203
Volunteers' Final Payment..................................202-203
Return to Alabama.. 203
Camps Herbert and Falkner..................................203-205
Muster Out... 205

ILLUSTRATIONS.

Frontispiece...Opp.
Maj. Tom. O. Smith.. "   16
Capt. Newman D. Lacy.. "   32
Maj. Henry B. Foster .... "   48
Maj. Robert B. DuMont .... "   64
Capt. E. H. Graves .... "   80
Capt. W. J. Vaiden.. "   96
Capt. J. D. Hagan... " 112
Lieut. Leon Schwarz... " 128
Lieut. Sherwood Bonner .... " 144
Breaking Camp at Spring Hill...................................... " 160
Maj. William W. Brandon... " 176
Maj. S. S. Pugh... " 192

ADDENDA.

It was with mingled delight and regret that the Alabamians doffed their uniforms and returned to civic habiliments. Warm friendships had been contracted during the six months' service and men were sorry to part with comrades whom they might never see again. But in the Second Alabama, the volunteers derived immense pleasure from an attestation of their esteem and affection for the man who, more than any one else, labored to obtain their muster out. An impressive ceremony was arranged at Camp Hilary A. Herbert where Major William W. Brandon was presented with a handsome, costly gold watch, chain and charm by the enlisted men of the regiment.

Private J. S. Hood, of Company F, started the movement to make the presentation and a committee was appointed to take up subscriptions as follows: Joseph R. Williams, Company A; Charles W. Holley, Co. L; J. S. Hood, Co F; Charles D. Faber, Co D; R. H. McWhorter, Co. E; Smith Dickens, Co. M; Sergt. W. A. McCreary, Co. B; R. E. Austill, Co. C; W. J. Malone, Co. H; Sergt. W. E Harris, Co. I; Sergt. W. T. Sheehan, Co. G; Corporal C. W. Jackson, Co. K.

Men who did not feel constrained by gratitude for Major Brandon's fight to have the regiment mustered out, were moved, by admiration for his ability, to contribute to the presentation fund. Major Brandon had so deeply impressed the men of the Second Alabama with his ability as an officer and his kindliness as a man that a marked eagerness was apparent on all sides to make eminently successful the presentation to him of a token of affection and esteem.

The watch, chain and charm were suitably engraved. Virgil Bouldin, a private in Company I, and ex-member of the state legislature, was selected to make the presentation speech. Major Brandon responded feelingly.

In the First Alabama, the officers showed their esteem for the soldierly excellence of Lieutenant Colonel McDonald by presenting him with a superb saber and scabbard. Lieutenant Colonel McDonald's fellow officers were lavish in their praise of his egregious ability as an officer; and his response to the presentation speech breathed a deep regard for the patriotism, loyalty and valor of Alabama.

Meanwhile, the rank and file of the First Regiment, under the impression that Colonel Higdon had fought single-handed for their muster out, showered on him a thousand evidences of their kindly regard.

Altogether, the two regiments disbanded amid innumerable circumstances of felicity.

* * * *

But the closing days of the Second Alabama's service were marked with intense disgust over the quality of food furnished. Both regiments were fed by contract during the few days prior to the muster out, but at Montgomery the men complained bitterly that the meats furnished were either tainted or practically uncooked.

* * * * *

BATTALION FORMATIONS.

FIRST ALABAMA.
  First Battalion—Companies K, L, A and G.
  Second Battalion—Companies H, D, M and I.
  Third Battalion—Companies C, E, F and B.

SECOND ADABAMA.
  First Battalion—Companies A, L, F and D.
  Second Battalion—Companies E, M, B and C.
  Third Battalion—Companies H, I, G and K.

* * *

CORRECTIONS AND ADDITIONS.

In Company A, Second Alabama, Captain H. B. May, a most promising officer, was elected to the captaincy from the Second Junior Lieutenancy, J. T. Bullen having been second lieutenant at the time.

The captaincy of Company M, Second Alabama, was filled, after the rejection of Captain Rowan, by Captain (incorrectly termed lieutenant) W. L. Pitts, of Selma, a lawyer whose capacities and possibilities as an officer won the respect of all who came to know him in the army.

The Lomax Rifles captured the first prize in the militia drill at Washington, D. C., in 1887, as related on page 73.

DEATH ROLL.

Frank J. Maloney, First Alabama (correction).

Sam Noble, Corporal Company D, First Alabama, died at Anniston, Ala., from typhoid fever while home on furlough.

Martin T. Whatley, Private, Company C, Second Alabama, died at Winn, Ala., while home on furlough.

G. Yawn, Private, Company G, Second Alabama, died September 28, at Graceville, Fla., while home on furlough.

William J. Murphy, Private, Company B, Second Alabama, died at Camp Hilary A. Herbert, October 21.

Men of The First Alabama.

Regimental Quartermaster Sergeant, Lewis W. Patteson.

COMPANY K.
Ranson, Edgar F.
Williams, John, Deserted.

COMPANY L.
John S. Hargrove, First Sergeant.
John H. Cook, Sergeant.
Corporal John J. Burnett.
Alexander H. Gratz, Corporal.
Oatts, John A.,
Owen, Walter V.,
Suttie, David.

COMPANY A.
2nd Lieut. Lucius C. Montgomery,
Sergt. Garland Kirven,
Corporal Samuel I. Bigham,
Bare, William A.,
Connally, John,
Creilly, Otto C.,
Ferrie, John T.,
Keirsey David D.,
Oesger, Frank,
Parrott, J. Frank,
Scoggins, Jerry M.

COMPANY G.
Sergt, L. S. Handley, Jr.,
Sergt. C. T. Thomasson,
Corporal Burlin R. Starnes,
Alred, Charles A.,
Bragdon, H. T.,
Bean, Alex W.,
Fillingin, Barney,
Fletcher, Frank M.,
Goodwin, Melvin,
Harris, Howard,
Hand, Eugene F.,
Hays, Charles,
Jennings, Charles,
Jollee, Edgar R,
Kimball, Rollin C.,
Kieling, Harry,
Meagher, James J.,
Pierce, P. B.,
Pickard, Tony,
Ray, Carl E.,
Shaw, O. W.,
Shilling, Frank,

Short, Marshall C.,
Venelle, Edward E.,
Walthall, H. B.,
Wooley, David Z.,

COMPANY H.
Corporal John Reily,
Donnell, John T.,
Edmondson, L. E.,
Edmundson, Joe,
Graham, Minor E.,
Rayborn, George,
Trenholm, C. V.,
Tussie, D. F.

COMPANY D.
Corporal Fred H. Rounsaville,
Boguskie, William,
Breadion, Wm., Deserted.

COMPANY M.
Palvado, C. J.,
Rooks, Robert R.,
Smithson, T. C.,

COMPANY I.
Corporal Postell Lewis,
Corporal Chas. P. Nunnelly, transferred.
Cosper, Clem A.,
Hense, Ed.,
Mason, Eillod L.,
McCullers, Burrell,
Skipper, James L.,

COMPANY C.
Burns, Henry W.,
Dorsett, Wm. L.,
Duran, Bud,

COMPANY E.
McBee, Henry R.,

COMPANY F.
Qmster. Sergt Hiram Burrow,
Sergt. Charles F. Schneider,
Musician Bernard R. Radford,
Bryant, W. L.,
Collette, J O,
Helveston, Laurin,
Mason, J Thomas,
Williams, Perry L.,
Reed, J. W.,

COMPANY E.
Arthur, G. P.,
Armistead, Gus.

Armistead, Ike,
Chambliss, Pomeroy,
Castile, Robert A.,
Green, H. J. S.,
Kalin, John,
Keebaugh, Ollie,
Legg, J. B.,
McDaniel, Thomas,
Pruitt, E. W.,
Rosson, W. M.,
Tompkins, Emmet J.,
Walters, Ulis,

Men of the Second Alabama.

COMPANY A.

Corporal Kearney W. McDade.
Burdeshaw, Marion C.,
Deal, Robert L.
Ledyard, Robert E.,
McKenzie, Alfred J.,
Matthews, Dessie,
Rawlinson, Douglas,
Smith, William R.,
Shider, Thomas B.,

COMPANY L.

Sergeant Bozeman C. Bulger.
Edwards, Locksley T.,
Harrison, Charles F.,
Johnston, Charles O.,

COMPANY F.

Sergt. Charles H. LaBoyteaux,
Booth, David W.,
Chisolm, Ernest J.,
Meredith, Reuben A.,
Powell, Hamerica H.,
Raburn, Luther W.,

COMPANY D.

Donaldson, A K,
Gullette, J. E.,
Lansdell, Charles B.,
Renfroe, Nathaniel D.,
Steed, Thomas G.,

COMPANY M.

Wagoner John C. Johnston,
Brodnax, Robert R.,

Harrison, Claude D.,
Howd, Pearl D.,
Linning, Charles, Dischgd.
Newsom, James.
Woolf, Eugene L.,

COMPANY B.

Corporal John D. Burnett, Jr.,
Broades, John.
Hendon, Edwin T., Jr.,

COMPANY C.

Corporal Frank O'Rourke,
Deckard, Thomas B.,
Faulk, Thomas F.,
Hubbird, Joseph F.,
Lamare, Vincent A.,
Stanford, Ed L.,
Tranum. Woods,
West, Wylie F,

COMPANY H.

Carter, Elias G.,
Turner, Ulysses H.,

COMPANY I.

Alfred W. McGan, Qmstr. Sergt.
Corporal William D. Keeton,
Corporal Charles Rice Coffey,
Elmore Kennamer, Musician,
Richard H. Smith, Wagoner,
Walter D. Green, Corporal.
Gullatt, John A,
Gober, Isaac,
Oden, Henry,
Sisk, Erskin M.,
Thrower, James M.,

COMPANY G.

Captain John R. Barr (resigned).
Sergeant W. M. Petry,
Harris, J. M.,
Kaigler, O G.,
McTyer, T. F.,
Stevens. L. M.,
Smith, W. T.,

COMPANY K.

Carlton, Walter S,
Jones, Edgar W,

www.ingramcontent.com/pod-product-compliance
Lightning Source LLC
Chambersburg PA
CBHW021813230426
43669CB00008B/741